True Life in God

Vassula

Volume Eight
(Notebook 71 - Notebook 79:28)

Original Handwriting Edition

Published by

Trinitas™

Declaration

The decree of the Congregation for the Propagation of the Faith, A.A.S. 58, 1186 (approved by Pope Paul VI on October 14, 1966) states that the Nihil Obstat and Imprimatur are no longer required on publications that deal with private revelations, provided they contain nothing contrary to faith and morals.

The publisher wishes to manifest unconditional submission to the final and official judgment of the Magisterium of the Church.

True Life in God
Vassula
Volume Eight   (Notebook 71 - Notebook 79:28)

Published by

Trinitas™
P.O. Box 475
Independence, Missouri, USA 64051
Phone (816) 254-4489
FAX (816) 254-1469

For further information direct all inquiries to Trinitas.

Cover photo: from Agamian Portrait, courtesy of Holy Shroud Guild.

Printed in United States of America.

Also available in Spanish, French, Italian, German, Croatian, Bulgarian, Mexican, Greek, Danish, Russian, Portuguese, Japanese, and other languages. For information contact Trinitas.

Table of Contents

Other Titles Available
True Life in God

Original Handwriting Edition	Printed Editions
My Angel Daniel	
Volume 1—NB 1-16	Volume 1—NB 1-31
Volume 2—NB 17-28	Volume 2—NB 32-58
Volume 3—NB 29-41	Volume 3—NB 59-63
Volume 4—NB 42-53	Volume 4—NB 64-71
Volume 5—NB 54-58	Volume 5—NB 71-79
Volume 6—NB 59-65:35	
Volume 7—NB 65:36-71:18	

Books Related to the Messages and Additional Publications

When God Gives a Sign, Vassula Ryden—Rene Laurentin
Prayers of Jesus and Vassula
Vassula of the Sacred Heart's Passion—Michael O'Carroll, C.S.Sp.
Bearer of the Light—Michael O'Carroll, C.S.Sp.
Fire of Love (Holy Spirit)—Michael O'Carroll, C.S.Sp.
John Paul II—Michael O'Carroll, C.S.Sp.

Welcome

To the praise of Jesus and Mary

Jesus asked me to tell you to always take my name, Vassula, out of the message and replace it with your own name.

I really must express here my gratitude to my family, my spiritual director, and all my faithful friends who have made the preparation of this book possible.

I want to mention Father René Laurentin, Sister Lucy Rooney, Father Bob Faricy, Father Michael O'Carroll, Tony Hickey, Pat Callahan, Tom Austin, and everyone who promotes and helps distribute these messages. I bless the Lord and thank Him for the ears that heard His Cry of Love from His Cross and now, touched, become His mouthpieces broadcasting this Cry of Love.

In Prayer
St. Michael, the Archangel

Sculptured in Sussex Oak by Claire Sheridan
Photo: Courtesy of Black Rock College, Dublin, Ireland

Introduction

Cardinal Kuharic Receives Vassula Ryden

Vassula and her spiritual counselor Father Michael O'Carroll were invited to Croatia in February 1995. During the visit they were received by the Archbishop of Zagreb, Cardinal Franjo Kuharic for an hour-long discussion. In his report Father O'Carroll wrote that after he had given the Cardinal his observations about the good fruits of Medjugorje, "His Eminence turned to Vassula and asked, 'And you, what have you to tell us about yourself?' She spoke to Cardinal Kuharic about her conversion, her mission, Church unity, Russia, the Orthodox Church, the present-day apostasy, as well as the revolt against tradition and the present Pope. The Cardinal said to her, 'You are like Saint Paul, and you declare the whole truth; the facts about the apostasy are exact.'

"The Cardinal was visibly impressed by Vassula's testimony," said Father O'Carroll. "While we were speaking, one of the Cardinal's photographers took several pictures and a journalist recorded everything we were saying. The Cardinal allowed photographs with Vassula's camera. Next day, several papers carried reports of the interview, obviously through the Cardinal's press office, quoting his words of approval and praise. Twice he blessed her, saying 'I bless you and your mission.'"

Following is a translation of one of the reports in the Croatian media, this one published February 3, 1995 in Zagreb's "Vercernji List," a respected Croatian daily newspaper:

Cardinal Kuharic Receives Mystic Vassula Ryden *Pleading For Christian Unity*

Zagreb - Zagreb's Archbishop, Cardinal Franjo Kuharic received yesterday in the Residence of the Archdiocese of Zagreb, in a private audience, Vassula Ryden of the Greek Orthodox Christian faith. During the last six years, she has become known around the world as an individual who personally receives messages from Jesus Christ. Vassula Ryden is visiting Croatia at the invitation of prayer groups from Djakova, Osijek and Zagreb who follow her spiritual messages. In the hour-long meeting with Vassula and her spiritual counselor, Irish priest Father O'Carroll, the mystic shared the content of her personal visions and messages. After their discussions, Cardinal Kuharic said that Vassula Ryden, by her own admission, was far from her religion, but she, like Saint Paul before Damascus, experienced fundamental conversion and became devout. She travels the world evangelizing for Christian unity; obedience to the Pope; veneration of the Eucharist; devotion to the Sacred Heart of Jesus; and especially, a Gospel morality of life; as well as for deep religious conversion of the world. Vassula Ryden has met with the Pope, with cardinals and with bishops around the world.

"This is a matter of private revelation and we allow her to speak because what she says conforms to Gospel truth," said Zagreb's Archbishop.

Following her visits to Djakova — where she was received by the Djakova-Srijem Bishop, Cyril Kos, — and Osijek where, in both cities, she spoke to packed churches about her personal mystical experience and Christ's messages, Vassula held a spiritual meeting yesterday afternoon in Zagreb's Globus Hall. She will visit Split and also go on a pilgrimage to Medjugorje.

Photograph of the article from "Vercernji List" (Evening News). Friday, February 3, 1995

KARDINAL FRANJO KUHARIĆ PRIMIO MISTIČARKU VASSULU RYDEN

Propovijeda jedinstvo kršćana

ZAGREB - Zagrebački nadbiskup kardinal Franjo Kuharić primio je jučer u Nadbiskupskom dvoru u Zagrebu u privatni posjet Vassulu Ryden, Grkinju pravoslavne vjere, koja je unatrag šest godina u svijetu poznata kao osoba koja osobno prima poruke od Krista. Vassula Ryden u Hrvatskoj boravi na poziv molitvenih skupina iz Đakova, Osijeka i Zagreba, koje slijede njezine duhovne poruke. Kardinal Kuharić zadržao se s Vassulom i njezinim duhovnim vođom, irskim svećenikom O'Carolom, u jednosatnom razgovoru, u kojem ga je mističarka upoznala sa sadržajem svojih osobnih viđenja i poruka. Nakon toga razgovora, kardinal Kuharić rekao je da je Vassula Ryden, po osobnom svjedočenju, bila daleko od vjere, ali je poput sv. Pavla pred Damaskom doživjela temeljito obraćenje i uzvjerovala. Ona putuje svijetom propovijedajući jedinstvo kršćana, poslušnost Papi kao učitelju vjere, čašćenje euharistije, pobožnost prema Srcu Isusovu, a osobito evanđeoski moral života, kao i temeljno obraćenje svijeta. Vassula Ryden susrela se i s Papom, kardinalima i biskupima u svijetu.

- Riječ je, dakle, o privatnoj objavi, a mi joj dopuštamo da govori, jer ono što govori u skladu je s evanđeoskom istinom - rekao je zagrebački nadbiskup.

Nakon Đakova, gdje ju je primio đakovačko-srijemski biskup Ćiril Kos, i Osijeka - u oba je grada u prepunim crkvama govorila o svojom osobnom mističnom iskustvu i Kristovim porukama svijetu - Vassula je jučer poslijepodne održala u dvorani »Globus« na Zagrebačkom velesajmu duhovni skup, a posjetit će i Split i hodočastiti u Medugorje. (IKA)

II

Vassula Ryden's Presentation to the
World Council of Churches

Unit I—Unity and Renewal

Consultation on Christian Spirituality for Our Times

27 April—4 May, 1994

Prayer: *Father, we consecrate ourselves in soul and body to Your service, so that Your eyes and Your heart never leave us.*
Set Your Royal Throne inside us and give us Your orders. Make us advance in purity of heart to accomplish all that You have given us.
Amen

God's Calling to His People
Vassula Ryden

Introduction

When I received the invitation to speak about my own way of living in Christ today, I was reluctant to put into words my particular "experience" with God. I do not dare to formulate a classified "spirituality" out of my own intimate "conversations with Jesus". Rather, I will leave the freedom of God who lifted up the prophets and who spoke and revealed Himself "in many and various ways" (Hebrews 1:1) to convey again His message through a weak hand, a member of Christ's Body. He poured out His Spirit upon all flesh (Acts 2:17) and I am one of the sons and daughters through whom He returns to respell His Blessed Word. In this sense what follows is a different kind of testimony of the mystical tradition of the undivided Church.*

Calling to Union in God

To be united and one with God we have to allow His Spirit to invade us. This is what He says:

Allow My Spirit to breathe and dwell in the depths of your soul. Leave Me free to shatter all impurities and imperfections that confront Me. I shall come like a tempest inside you and carry out the decision of My Heart...In order to prepare you for this perfect union, I need to purify you and adorn your soul. I would have to bend My bow and set you as a target for My arrow. Oh what will I not do for you!

---

*My testimonies were published under the general title: *True Life in God.*

Allow My Spirit to augment in you and My Divine Fire to roar in your soul. You will be molten under the action of My Divine Fire. Do not lament then when I come to you like a hammer shattering your imperfections. Do not ask your Holy One: What is He doing? I am on My way to the inner room, My Dwelling Place, and persistent blocks will not stop Me from proceeding. I shall burst them all with a tempest. I shall devour these rivals...

I want to make out of you a docile instrument since My presence will be felt inside you like a fire and like an arrow. Do not fear. I shall not break you. I shall only break My rivals. I shall only be combatting inside you. I shall also be mindful of your frailty...

So allow your King to rule over you, allow your Sovereign to reign over you...Every little impurity will be seiged by My purity and annihilated, and My Light shall continue to glow inside you, and My Spirit shall flow in your spirit like a river...(20.1.92).

Calling to Hallow God's Name

Since the foundations of the earth I have called you by your name. But when I proposed peace, universal peace, nearly all of you were for war. Yet I am pouring out My Holy Spirit <u>now</u>, to remind you of your true foundations and that <u>all</u> of you are My seed—but today My seed is filled up with dead words...

Generation, you have still not set your minds for Me—when will you decide to return to Me? Do you want to pass this era's threshold by blazing fire, by brimstone and devouring flame? <u>Ask for your daily bread, and I shall give it to you!</u>

Beware of them who keep up the outward appearance of religion but reject the inner power of it. The inner power that is My Holy Spirit.... Place your ear on My mouth, this mouth that breathed in you through your nostrils: <u>life</u>, and from the dust of the soil, I revived you to conquer the earth. I touched you, and asked you to listen to My Word since then. Come, you must set your heart right. Renounce the iniquities that stain your soul and with all your heart, <u>Hallow My Name</u>.

Calling to Follow Christ in His Way

I am going to save My people and I will take men and women from every nation, every race and every language by their sleeve and ask them:

"Do you want to follow Me?" And they will say: "We want to go with You, since we have now learnt the truth."

And I will bring one after the other back to live in My Heart! Who is there to pity My people if it is not Me? When hordes of nations fall continuously into apostasy and the crown of terror is on every head and when debauchery is ruling their heart, how can I remain silent? Godlessness has spread throughout the world. Am I to remain silent?

Happy is the heart who will make peace with his brother, for he will be called, child of the Most High.

Happy is the heart who will stop wandering in the night and will reconcile truly with his brother. Not only will he enjoy My favour, but I will reveal to him the inexhaustible riches of My Sacred Heart so that people around him, astounded by his radiant beauty will say, "Truly, God is hidden within him." (3.2.93)

I have stepped out of My Throne to come all the way into your room to court you and remind you that you are heirs to My Kingdom; I have stepped out of My Dwelling Place and have taken the wilderness in search of you...to honour My Name I have roused the dead to preach to you My Kingdom...

Tell Me, who of you will be first to end My agony and My groans for unity and peace before the hour comes? This hour that leaves all My angels trembling...

Who among you is the soul who will grain the nations with seeds of love and peace?...

Who of you all will be the first to place his feet into My blood-stained footprints? Are you sincerely seeking Me?

I am sending you, creation, messenger after messenger to break through your deafness, but I am weary now of your resistance and your apathy. I am weary of your arrogance and your inflexibility when it comes to assemble for unity...My Church is in ruin because of your division. (Only a few are) applying My advice and are practicing My desires...(18.2.93)

Calling to Receive the Gifts of the Holy Spirit

My Spirit comes with full force in these days to help you now when night is yawning its darkness all around you. (24.1.91)

The inner power of My Church is My Holy Spirit in it, alive and active, like a heart in a body. My Holy Spirit is the heart of My body which is the Church. (15.4.91)

My Holy Spirit is the fire which bends and melts hearts to follow My instructions, turning away your eyes from pointless images. My Holy Spirit is the generous giver of My Words, making your whole mind and heart seek for wisdom. Wholeheartedly entreat for the gifts of My Holy Spirit, especially in these times. He will be your torch to rescue you from death and your feet from stumbling. Oh! What would My Holy Spirit not do for you!

My Holy Spirit will lead you to pass your life in My presence and in the courts of My Kingdom.

My Holy Spirit is essential to reconstruct My Church. He is the corner-stone of My Church, but your era is rejecting it.... I tell you again, the builders are there, but they have to be formed and instructed. Hurry and rebuild My Church by using every stone, but do not forget the essential; do not reject the cornerstone! (11.6.93)

An Appeal for Reconciliation: A Common Date for Easter

Today again in these days of Lent, I come to you, to ask you for reconciliation. Go and reconcile with your brother, for in reconciling with him you are reconciling with Me your God. Offer Me your peace, as I offer you My peace. Imitate Me and be holy. (10.3.90)

I have taken your faults on myself, I have reconciled you to the Father and My life I laid down for you. So, what could I have done more that I have not done? (20.1.92)

I desire My children united. Realize the gravity of your division, the urgency of My call and the importance of My request. All I ask is love to break the barriers of your division. (20.10.91)

And now, I make a special appeal to all those who are under My Name and are working for unity and peace. I ask you to come to Me like a child and face Me answering these questions:

Brothers, have you done everything you can to preserve the unity of My body? (10.3.90)

Will I, brother, one more season go through the pain I have been going through year after year? Or will you give Me rest this time? Am I to drink one more season the cup of your division? Or will you rest My body and unify for My sake the Feast of Easter? In unifying the date of Easter, you will alleviate My pain, brother, and you will rejoice in Me and I in you and I will have the sight of many restored. (14.10.91)

Has anyone lowered his voice to hear Mine?

Who is the first righteous man among you who will decline and fade away so that My presence be seen? (25.10.91)

When will you all pass a decree by unanimous vote to celebrate the Feast of Easter all in one date? (21.12.92)

Unless you allow Me to uproot all that is not Me in your heart, you will never see how My Holy Spirit seeks in you more than any time: reconciliation and unity. I have shown you how to unite. Unity will be in your heart. Reconciliation will be in the heart and not by a signed treaty!

Will I hear from you your cry of surrender and of repentance? (14.9.92)

I do not want administrators in My House. They will not be justified in My Day because it is these very ones who have industrialized My House. (14.10.91)

I am shouting and I am trying to break through your deafness to save you, and if I reproach you, it is because of the greatness of the love I have for you. (14.10.91)

The coming of My reign on earth is at hand and My Will shall be done as it is in Heaven, and in your hearts I shall rebuild the unity of My Church...

I shall be with you all again and My priestly prayer to the Father shall be fulfilled. You shall be one like us, in the Holy Trinity (2.5.91)

An Invitation

Ms. Vassula Ryden was invited to attend the World Council of Churches' Consultation on Spirituality for Our Times that was held in Iasi, Romania, 25 April to 5 May 1994, hosted by Metropolitan Daniel of Moldavia and Bukovina Strada Stefan cel Mare 16, 6600 Iasi, Romania.

Additional Articles and Excerpts

Why Do We Receive Private Revelations If We Already Have the Full Revelation Through Christ?

Father Dr. Michael Kaszowski

According to Church teaching we have already received the entire revelation through Christ. But, even though we have the fullness of truth in Jesus, we need additional help in order to understand it completely. The Holy Spirit is that help for us. Jesus said that He would remind us of the Truth Revealed, help us discover its meaning and show us things to come: "But the Counsellor, the Holy Spirit, whom the Father will send in My Name, will teach you all things and will remind you of everything I have said to you" (J14:26).

The work of reminding, leading to the truth and announcing things to come did not end after the New Testament was completed. The Holy Spirit has continued His work in the Church — work manifested also through the gift of prophecy. This gift allows those who possess it to become the witnesses of God, the advocates of His truth and love, and thus to call us to demonstrate to our Creator our own love for Him.

St. Paul considers the gift of prophecy as the most important for the Church (1 Cor 14:1): "Follow the way of love and eagerly desire spiritual gifts, especially the gift of prophecy". He places the prophets straight after the apostles and ahead of teachers: "And in the Church God has appointed first of all apostles, second prophets, third teachers..."(1 Cor 12:28, comp. Eph 3:5, 4:11). He talks about the Church being built upon the apostles and prophets (Eph 2:20) "...built on the foundation of the apostles and prophets, with Christ Jesus himself as the chief cornerstone".

The prophecy of Joel says: "And afterwards—says the Lord—I will pour out My Spirit on all people. Your sons and daughters will prophesy, your old men will dream dreams, your young men will see visions. Even on My servants, both men and women, I will pour out My Spirit in those days" (Joel 2:28-29).

But this "forgotten" gift is granted under various guises more often than we think. Its most common form is inner enlightenment - understanding of a Revealed Truth, a passage of the Bible, for example, during a Bible study meeting, a discussion, or a sermon. Another less common gift of prophecy is private revelation. Private revelations are used by the Holy Spirit to remind us of God's Word, lead us towards the truth and show us the future. For example, the children from La Salette, Lourdes, and Fatima received the gift of prophecy in an exceptional form; they became the tools through which God enriched His Church.

The revelations of Fatima are an example of the importance of the prophetic function for the good of the Church and all mankind. Through the events at Fatima the Holy Spirit reminded us of the long-revealed truth about God's readiness to show mercy, of His compassion and fairness, of the value of conversion and repentance. The Holy Spirit enriched the Church through the understanding of the value of celebrating the first Saturdays of the month. The Holy Spirit revealed the future at Fatima; that mankind would be punished if it did not repent. It was God's will to use children from a small village to remind the Church's servants to consecrate the world, and especially Russia, to the Immaculate Heart of Mary.

Fatima has not diminished the importance of Public Revelation. It is not competing with the Holy Bible. Nothing of the Church was taken away. Instead, a most valuable redemptive truth was imparted: offer everything through the Heart of Mary, be at Her service and you will be at the service of God; offer reparation for sins. This simple reminder from Fatima was a tremendous gift to the Church.

The many mystical experiences we hear about occurring all around the world, particularly Marian apparitions, tell us that the gift of prophecy has not died down; it is in fact increasing because God's wisdom has declared this gift as particularly necessary in the twentieth century.

In spite of the existence of the Bible we constantly need reminders about the Truth Revealed and of our own destiny. We are immersed in a world where we do not see God or the supernatural, so we need constant reminders of Him, of His love for us and of our final destiny to live with Him forever in His house.

Prophecy in the form of private revelations helps us toward redemption and does not threaten the Holy Bible. On the contrary, private revelations encourage Bible reading, meditation and deeper understanding of scripture. Private revelations would not be authentic if they resulted in displacing Bible reading. **Authentic private revelations lead to hunger for God's Word.**

Those unwilling to accept private revelations certainly would not reject the need for sermons, conferences, or reading theology because there already exists one revelation, one Holy Scripture and the body of Church teaching. When we put the Holy Scripture as first and most important we do not at the same time say that there is no value in sermons. We acknowledge that these do not contradict or substitute for the Holy Bible but deepen our appreciation of it.

No believer has to choose between accepting public or private revelations, just as the faithful need not choose between the Holy Bible, Tradition or the Magisterium of the Church.

There is no need to oppose those things that mutually enrich each other since they all have the same source: the Holy Spirit. "There are different kinds of gifts but the same Spirit. There are different kinds of service but the same Lord. There are different kinds of working, but the same God works all of them in all men. Now to each one of the manifestation of the Spirit is given for the common good" (1 Cor 12:4-7).

There is need for caution but it should foremost guard against errors, not prevent the authentic voice of the Lord being heard. When the Lord speaks, man should fall on his knees and listen and change his life. We must not be caught saying: "Why is God speaking now when He has already said everything in the past?".

A cautious person, as St. Paul says (Thes 5:19), will not put out the Spirit's fire. We must not ignore the hand of God extended towards us nor His Mother's for we would be wounding their love for us. We must not prevent others either from receiving the grace of God as Jesus himself warns saying: "Woe to you, teachers of the law and Pharisees, you hypocrites! You shut the Kingdom of Heaven in men's faces. You yourself do not enter, nor will you let those enter who are trying to".

And what of the false prophets? The Holy Scripture warns us of false prophets.

But the same Holy Scripture announces the multitude of prophets (Acts 2:17-21) and, at the same time, opposition towards prophecy in the Church (Zech 13:3-4).

There will, therefore, be authentic and false prophets. The authentic prophets will be persecuted (Luke 6:26). So, it will be necessary to thoroughly examine every prophet. Jesus gave us instructions how to recognize the genuine prophets, for His prophets will bring good fruit.

The history of the Church teaches us a wonderful lesson. Were the many schisms and errors perpetrated by private revelations or were they the creation of theologians basing their theories on their own ideas? We can equally ask today whether the current attitudes in the Church, such as questioning the authority of the Pope, rejecting the sacrament of reconciliation and adoration of the Blessed Sacrament, rejecting the Eucharist as the perpetual sacrifice, disappearance of the cult of Our Lady and other saints. Are all these problems a result of private revelations or do they originate from other sources?

Private revelations today call for the return of all those traditions of the Church which somehow have been put aside. Isn't the private revelation revealed to Vassula thus given in order to open our eyes?

Father Dr. Michael Kaszowski teaches at the Seminary in Katowice, Poland.

Vassula: An Eyewitness Speaks
The Tree and Its Fruits

In addition to the transformation in Vassula's own life, I would like to note that her writings have given rise to many serious and profound conversions among the lukewarm and those who were quite far from the faith. It is well to note that it is the fruit that is the criterion that Jesus lays down for judging the quality of a tree. Genuine conversions can only be produced by the grace of God (**"Without Me you can do nothing"**). A genuine conversion which is balanced, deep, and lasting cannot be produced by any psychological techniques, and anyone like Vassula whose ministry produces large numbers of sincere, lasting, and well–balanced conversions has passed the test that the Lord himself has set down for judgment: we know the tree by its fruits.

It seems evident to me that what Jesus so severely denounced in Matthew 12:24 was a stubborn resistance before strong evidence that God was acting to save His people. It was the spirit of the Pharisees and Sadducees, and it seems to be the spirit of our age. The Sadducees were the rationalists of their age and thus enemies of the supernatural. Their successors are the rationalists of our own age. The Pharisees had bound God into their own system of thought, so much so that He lost all freedom (to their way of thinking) of acting as He saw fit. Their successors are, like the Pharisees, sometimes apparently model Christians, but somehow at some point in their development their openess to new graces comes to an end. Just as there were these two tendencies in the time of Christ, these same tendencies exist today, and we all may be prone to either or both at

XI

some point. Those who combat Vassula and mystics of our time are usually following these tendencies.

There are the new Sadducees who reject all that is supernatural, and there are the new Pharisees who reach a certain juncture, maybe at Fatima, maybe at Garabandal, maybe at Medjugorje, but thereafter they are unable to listen to what God is saying to His people now.

I feel that the evidence in favor of Vassula is very strong, and so I would urge especially those of us who are tempted to follow the Pharisees to avoid any hasty action. In moral theology we are taught that it is wrong to act in doubt. We cannot attack a mystic when in our own conscience we have come to realize that the question might be more complex than we had first realized, and that maybe we are dealing with the genuine mystic. In the Acts of the Apostles, we read of a wise Pharisee at the time of the early Church who, though a Jew, realized the need for caution in dealing with possible revelations from God. He said, "If this enterprise, this movement of theirs, is of human origin, it will break up of its own accord but if it does in fact come from God, you will not only be unable to destroy them, but you might find yourselves fighting against God." (Acts 5:38-39)

I therefore urge those of us who have come to realize that Vassula may, in fact, be a prophet for our times to pray, fast and reflect—in any event, to avoid spreading rumors or engaging in attacks. As time goes by, this matter will become clearer and clearer with each passing day.
(Extract from an article by Father James Fannan, P.I.M.E., Vassula's first spiritual advisor)

On The Discernment of Mystical Phenomena: The Credibility of Vassula Ryden

Father Michael O'Carroll, who is presently Vassula's spiritual counselor, is adequately qualified and competent in the area of ascetical and mystical theology and can therefore be trusted.

This devout priest has written the following:

"I have studied very seriously the case of Vassula Ryden. I have read her writings attentively...I have consulted well-informed priests who know her...My firm opinion is that she is a precious instrument of God for a ministry which is much needed: that of the Sacred Heart of Jesus."

For all persons who are free of prejudice and able to judge objectively, the testimony of Fr. O'Carroll should inspire great reassurance. His qualifications in theology and spirituality are impressive. In fact, he obtained a doctorate after having supported a thesis on spiritual direction. He has supplied twenty-five articles for the Dictionary of Spirituality and he is the author of many books, among which are five theological encyclopedias. He has given conferences in many countries; he is a member of the Pontifical Marian Academy, a member of the French Society of Marian Studies, and an associate of the Bollandists of Brussels.

Consequently, it can be said that Vassula Ryden is in "moral security" under the spiritual counselling of Fr. O'Carroll. His obvious competence should suffice to dispel the doubts of those who blindly and violently attack Vassula Ryden and her writings.

Furthermore, Vassula Ryden has the support of Fr. René Laurentin who has studied a great many extraordinary supernatural phenomena presently occurring throughout the world. For my part, having studied ascetical and mystical theology both in theory and in practice over more than fifty years, I do not hesitate to stand alongside the two "experts" mentioned above and with the many priests who know Vassula Ryden and her writings very well and who have faith in her.... Moreover, Vassula Ryden has a strict right to her reputation, as Canon Law reminds us. "No one is allowed to attack in any illegitimate manner anyone's good reputation." (Can. 220) We cannot with impunity before God and man destroy the reputation of mystics...they have a right to be treated justly...and also charitably.

Charismatic powers are not pure human or ecclesiastic inventions but they were conferred by Christ Himself upon His first disciples and also upon all believers: **"These signs will accompany those who believe. In My name they will drive out demons, they will speak new languages...They will lay hands on the sick and they will recover."**

Therefore, no one has the right to doubt this conferring of charism by Our Lord, for the words of the Gospel just quoted leave no room for ambiguity and are not debatable.

Without neglecting the virtue of **prudence** which must obviously be equally **positive** and **negative**, it is appropriate to dispel fear of the extraordinary in the supernatural, a priori. **We must cease calling our fear "prudence", and our skepticism "wisdom".**

(Extract from an article by Father Ovila Melancon, C.S.C. of Montreal, Canada)

"Be Not Afraid"...*The first words of the pontificate of John Paul II*

Prayers Given to Vassula

Jesus to Vassula
January 29, 1990

Lord my God,
lift my soul from this darkness
into Your Light,
envelop my soul into Your
Sacred Heart,
feed my soul with Your Word,
anoint my soul
with Your Holy Name,
make my soul ready to
hear Your discourse,
breathe Your sweet fragrance
on my soul, reviving it,
ravish my soul
to delight Your Soul,
Father, embellish me, Your child,
by distilling Your pure myrrh
upon me,

You have taken me to Your
Celestial Hall,
where all the Elect are seated,

You have shown me around
to Your angels, ah,
what more does my soul ask?

Your Spirit has given me life
and You, who are the living
Bread have restored my life,
You have offered me to drink
Your Blood,
to be able to share for eternity
with You, Your Kingdom
and live forever and ever,

Glory be to the Highest!
Glory be to the Holy of Holies.
Praised be Our Lord.
Blessed be Our Lord, for His
Mercy and His Love
reaches from age to age
and forever will;
Amen.

Mary to Vassula
May 15, 1990

Father all Merciful,
let those who hear and hear again
yet never understand,
hear Your Voice this time and
understand that it is You
the Holy of Holies;
open the eyes of those who see
and see, yet never perceive, to
see with their eyes this time
Your Holy Face and Your Glory,
place Your Finger on their heart
so that their heart may open
and understand Your Faithfulness,

I pray and ask you all these
things Righteous Father,
so that all the nation be
converted and be healed through
the Wounds of Your Beloved Son,
Jesus Christ; Amen.

Prayers Jesus Recommended to Vassula
(to be said daily)

Novena of Confidence to the Sacred Heart

O Lord, Jesus Christ,
to Your Most Sacred Heart
I confide this intention (state
your request).

Only look upon me,
then do what Your Heart
inspires,
Let Your Sacred Heart decide,
I count on It, I trust in It,
I throw myself on Its Mercy.

Lord Jesus, You will not fail me.
Sacred Heart of Jesus,
I trust in Thee.
Sacred Heart of Jesus,
I believe in Thy love for me.
Sacred Heart of Jesus,
Thy Kingdom come.

O Sacred Heart of Jesus,
I have asked for many favors,
but I earnestly implore this one.
Take it. Place it in Thy Sacred
Heart.

When the Eternal Father sees it
covered with Thy Precious
Blood,
He will not refuse it.
It will be no longer my prayer,
but Thine, O Jesus.

O Sacred Heart of Jesus,
I place my trust in Thee.
Let me never be confounded.
Amen.

Prayer to St. Michael

St. Michael, the archangel,
defend us in the day of battle;
be our safeguard against the
wickedness and snares of the
devil.

May God rebuke him, we
humbly pray, and do thou,
O prince of the heavenly host,
by the power of God, cast into
hell, Satan, and all the other evil
spirits, who prowl through the
world seeking the ruin of souls.
Amen.

The Memorare of St. Bernard

Remember, O most gracious
Virgin Mary, that never was
it known that anyone who fled
to your protection, implored
your help, or sought your
intercession, was left unaided.

Inspired with this confidence,
I fly unto you.
O Virgin of Virgins,
my Mother!
To you I come, before you
I stand sinful and sorrowful.
O Mother of the Word
Incarnate, despise not my
petitions, but in your mercy,
hear and answer me.
Amen.

XIV

Excerpts from Notebook 71

13 April 94, NB p.4 . . . If We Do Not Hurry , The Earth Will Be Totally Ravaged

✠ My prophet's word...burns like fire and no hypocrite likes it

✠ Life is more powerful than Death and Love is more powerful than Evil because My Spirit is their Holy Companion

✠ Oh! If you only knew how powerful and what splendor your prayers can be if they come from your heart!

15 April 94, NB p.12 . . . Every Remembrance Of Me Pleases Me

19 April 94, NB p.12 . . . I Said To My Celestial Court: I Will Light A Fire Inside Her Soul

✠ Through you I have consumed with My fire many other souls

✠ I will...lead one by one out into the wilderness where I will speak to their heart

✠ You will only prove over and over again you come from Me by the great fortitude I will pour in you

10 May 94, NB p.18 . . . Allow Me To Progress You Into Sanctity

✠ He has revealed His face to you and released you from your captivity

18 May 94, NB p. 20 . . . Your Wealth Is Me

✠ I am your Peace

✠ I have offered you this unique gift to come to Me...never weary of writing

20 May 94, NB p.22 . . . With Me, Your Traits Will Be Mine

✠ Would a flower refuse water from its keeper?

21 May 94, NB p.23 . . . We Have Only A Mile To Go

✠ I will continue to make your adversaries retreat before you

✠ If you only knew how many demons have fled by the very sight of My Light

26 May 94, NB p.29 . . . Keep My Rules Securely

✠ My arm still has to shatter a few more rocks in you

27 May 94, NB p.3♭ . . . Now That I Have Resurrected You...Let Your Thoughts Be Heavenly Thoughts

✠ I have asked the Father to vest you with Myself

30 May 94, NB p.38 . . . You Must Intercede For The East And The West To Meet And Join Their Heart Into One

✠ I will unleash a torrential rain of fire on this earth...but I will rescue My people

31 May 94, NB p.43 . . . Unite The Dates Of Easter

✠ The more time passes for them to unite the dates of Easter, the more severe will be the sentence this generation will receive

✠ One section of My Church has been blinded

✠ My Return is imminent and woe to the unrepentant heart!

✠ Those who keep My Traditions will draw life from Them

2 June 94, NB p.54 . . . I Allow My Images To Weep

✠ Others, upon seeing the torrents shed...remain untouched...having lost the sense of My wonders...and with frenzy persecute My signs

✠ Our Two Hearts will defeat the enemy...I shall renew the face of the earth

✠ Tolerate your adversaries with love...they bring you closer to Me

3 June 94, NB p.62 . . . I Am Here To Warn The World

✠ You read My Messages but fail to understand the Heart of the Message

✠ Stay awake, praying...for the strength to survive all that is going to happen

generation, to this day, very few understood My Will .... generation, you are still
filled with spite; abide in My Light and
you will abide in Love; remain in My
Love and you will bear fruit in My
Love; see? how the Spirit of Truth
flashes in the sky His Light? but,
so many of you have not understood
what this text in the Scriptures means:
" it was the stone rejected by the builders
that became the keystone;*" have I not

---

* Ps 118:22

2

said that anyone who falls on that stone
will be dashed to pieces; anyone it falls on
will be crushed?* do not lose the state
of grace you had entered once by considering yourselves righteous, no man is
good except God .... do not judge the
sinner saying: " he knows nothing of the
way of peace nor of righteousness." leave
these things for Me; I am the only
judge ♡ ask Me to look after you and
I will; your petitions will carry to the

* Lk 20:18

3

clouds; ask! and I will save you ....
Mercy is at your doors, never doubt of
My Love; I bless you all leaving the
Sigh of My Love on your forehead ♡
IXΘΥΣ 🐟

13. 4. 94

yes! My Vassula, when I call, I touch
your heart! * it is I, Yahweh, lean on Me
and do not fear; My Heart is an Abyss
of Love and Tenderness; hear Me: the grass

* When I receive a call, I feel in my heart
a special great joy, an eagerness to rush
quickly to God, abandon everything and answer
His Call.

4

dries up, the turf all will wither, soon nothing will remain green anymore; if we do not hurry the earth will be totally ravaged; so few survivors are left now ... * do not believe those who prophesy saying: " all is well now, peace is already sprouting among you; " I have not sent these prophets, yet they are prophesying in blood to nations that eat the bread of wickedness; My prophet's word coming from My Mouth burns like fire

* Yahweh speaks in metaphors,

5

and no hypocrite likes it; My word
pronounced, shatters, like a hammer
it pounds on coarsened hearts shattering
them; no, how can I say that peace
is starting to bud when your lands are
imbued in iniquity and the corpses
ravaged by worm, how can I say
that love has moved your hearts when
your tongues are forked uttering blasphemies
on My Spirit? your lands are full
of prostitution*, no, they do not honour

* The Father means religious infidelity.

6

Me as their Father but dishonour Me without ceasing .... and the night has covered you without you noticing it; it creeped on the entire earth like death; how then am I to say, "you are glorifying My Name?" how am I to say, "you are hallowing My Name?" when your entire being is night? I am sending angel following close to angel to echo My words and pierce through your deafness, ah.... but so many of you judge them by human standards, because nothing is

7

penetrating you due to your coarsened heart; indeed the hour is here when Death is persecuting Life; you drive out from your premises, which in fact are Mine, My angels, abusing them, treating them like imposters and ever so savage- ly you try to kill their spirit along with My Spirit, thinking you are doing a holy duty for Me; but you will have no power over them, for the words they pronounce are Life and Life is stronger than Death, and Love is

8

more powerful than Evil because My Spirit
is their Holy Companion accompanying them;
so wherever My angels go, My Spirit is
with them; the Message I uttered
from the beginning was to love one
another, reconcile in My Love, to live
holy and hallow My Name; this is
still My Message, but ah, so few of you
have listened and followed it ....
– why do you still hang on to this
passing world? I have taught you not
to worry about your life; would I not

9

care for your needs *? I would adorn your soul if you would only let Me; from the time this Message went out I never stopped calling you to return to Me and change your lives; I have been asking you for amendments, for repentance, for vigils of prayers; I have been asking you for incense, incense from your heart, oh! if you only knew how powerful and what splendour your prayers can be if they come from your heart! your prayers

* Allusion to Mt 6:25

10

can destroy every evil empire in this world, they can uproot evil and break the ten horns* devouring now the earth together with My children; your prayers can over-power evil forces, although these forces are powerful, your incense *2 can purify this world; I tell you, grant yourselves no rest lest you be tested; be vigilant as never before; I will not desert you, I am with you all; I am with you to give you strength so that your breath

---

* 10 blasphemies against the 10 Commandments, of God. *2 prayers from the heart,

11

does not fail you; I am with you seedlings of Mine, and am only waiting to
be gracious to you and transplant you
in My garden of delights; see, I
Myself am taking up your cause to make
sure you are not devoured by the Enemy;
– and you, My daughter, allow Me
to use you as My weapon; I shall use
you to strike the evil kingdoms of this
world and he who governs them; Wisdom
will instruct you; accomplish your
daily duties; I, Yahweh bless you;

12

your Father and your Abba is near you;

A☧Ω

15. 4. 94

(I rushed just to be again, even for a few
seconds, with God. I came running to
Him.)

Illustrious Majesty: I love You.

ah Vassula, every remembrance of Me pleases
Me .... I, Yahweh, bless you My child and
My Own; I am your Resource ... and
Yahweh is My Name; A☧Ω

19. 4. 94

Feed me with Your words Lord, for I
am sick with love for You.

13

Vassula of My Sacred Heart, I said to
My Celestial Court: "I will light a fire
inside her soul, consume her and make
her Mine;" see? I have now conquered
your heart and through you I have consumed with My fire many other souls;
I have conquered them all! * I have
not used ferocity nor have I taken anyone
by force; I have only taken your hearts
with a glance and with a spark from

* Jesus' Voice reached a high note, showing His
excitement and joy.

14

My Heart; I have said to My Father, to your Holy Mother, to the saints and to all the denominations of My Angels :

" I intend to cover their frightful naked-ness with My Love, but first I will have to lure this generation and lead one by one out into the wilderness where I will speak to their heart; I Myself shall save My children, then all mankind shall know that I, Jesus, am your Saviour ; " keep faithful to Me and honour Me, My child; I have power to destroy all My

15

enemies see? Vassula let Me free to tell you what I contain in My Heart, listen, I heard you tell fr. O'Carroll that you wished to die as a martyr and how you earnestly wished to progress into sanctity; because, My friend, you are inviting Me at your table, I, in My turn, will grant your wish and honour you to drink from My Cup again and again; your wish will save you and many others; fear not, I will repay you later on; the Enemy's captives will be snatched away whenever you

16

will sip from My Cup; Vassula, love Me,
and for the sake of your love you have
for Me, I will strike the evil empires
together with he who reigns over them,
and they will tumble like rocks; love Me
and for the sake of your love I will
summon the Churches to unify the dates
of Easter; love Me and for your sake,
I will substitute this darkness for light
faster than foreseen; the fruit I
want from you is love! with your
love I can grant many prayers, so....

17

allow your adversaries to take you for an imposter although you come from Me, allow them to tear on you like enraged wolves,* what does it matter? you will only prove over and over again you come from Me by the great fortitude I will pour in you in these times of suffering

———————

* Jesus had stopped there, changed subject, smiled and said:

" do you enjoy being with Me in this way My child?" I said: 'Yes and how Lord!'

" I love you to folly...."

'Me too my Lord....'

18

and anyway, this portion will be one way
to lead you on the road you desired
to be this morning: the road to sanctification; My Own Love is beyond
all knowledge, learn from Me and be one
with Me ♡ come; ΙΧΘΥΣ ⟨°⟩

10. 5. 94

Lord?

I Am; feel loved by Me; allow Me to
progress you into sanctity; pray and ask;
happy are you who are instructed
by My Spirit; rejoice and be glad!

19

for the Kingdom of Heaven is not given
to just anyone, the Kingdom of Heaven
is given to the poor, to the simple
and to those My Father chooses; —
I prayed for you, Vassula, to obtain
from the Father His Graces and I
obtained them for you! since then,
you have seen the Dawn; ah...
yes! He has revealed His Face to you
and released you from your captivity;
and now, I shall take your fruits
and offer them to Him; flower,

20

remain in Me, and trust Me ; your Saviour , Jesus Christ will obtain mercy for you from the Father ; come !

ΙΧΘΥΣ 🐟

Greece – St Michael's island – Simi – Monastery of Panormiti.

18. 5. 94

Lord ?

I Am ; ecclesia shall revive ; allow Me to use your hand ; My Love is a jealous love that has no limits , see ? I want to be victorious in you , so do not break My commands : I have said, My daughter, that your wealth is Me ; your life

21

is Me, your joy is Me; I am your Peace; remain for a while with Me; I have offered you this unique gift to come to Me, so My Vassula, stop wriggling in My Hands*, you will only produce ripples in this stream of Peace in which you are immersed; daughter, be faithful in your love and I tell you again, never weary of writing; come

I Χ Θ Υ Σ

---

* When I do not go to Him daily to write and use my gift, the Lord reprimands me.

22

Panormiti - 20.5.94

peace be with you;

without Me you will live like the world, with Me you will live like in Heaven; without Me your traits will become those of the world, but with Me your traits will be Mine; remain in Me; rooted in Me, never neglect your gift, have Me as first and grant Me your time; would a flower refuse water from its keeper? so it is with you; do not refuse or neglect My Spirit who is the Living Water in you, keeping you alive; feel blessed for I have you

23

blessed; I bless you both*; ask Saint
Michael My Archangel to intercede for you,
for unity and for peace in the world,
come; I X Θ Y Σ

Panormiti 21. 5. 94

Vassula of My Sacred Heart write: peace
be with you, in Me you will live, so
delight in My Presence*², let your soul be
refreshed in My Presence; come and listen
to My Heart's desires: for the sake of the
love I have for you both*³, are you still

---

* Fr. Michael O'Carroll who was in this retreat
with me. *² In the Eucharist, *³ Fr. O'Carroll & I.

24

willing to follow in My stride? are you willing to sacrifice your time for My Interests? are you ready to crown My Plan* with success so that all Heaven with joy hails My victory? are you willing to respond to My needs with fervour and anxiety to please Me, your Saviour? if you allow Me to use you, I will invest your soul with My Divinity, with My Splendour, with My Seal .... we have only a mile to go My friends,

* Part of His Plan is:
True Life in God, messages of salvation, yes!

25

only a mile longer .... I have asked for your time and you have given it to Me! I have asked for your life and you have so generously offered it to Me!* I have girded you with My Strength to go forward with My Message   and you have', for this I will continue to make your adversaries retreat before you; have you been scathed by anyone? ah! if you only knew, how many demons have fled by the very sight

* Jesus in saying this, was very touched and I understood His emotion from the tone of His Voice and the slight shake of His Head.

26

of My Light...* I have given you My Light.... I promise you that I will not desert you, be constant in your prayers and let your lips repeat all that I have given you; renew your vows of faithfulness to Me and I will give you enough strength to follow Me and continue to consolidate My Church! Jesus is My Name and I bless you; I love you, love Me ♡ IΧΘΥΣ ⊃—◦

---

* Jesus stopped for a few seconds, and looked at me with very grave Eyes and told me what followed very gravely.

27

Just a few seconds after, the Father spoke:

Vassula, elevate your soul to Me; it is I,
Yahweh; your King is speaking; bless My Holy
Name and you shall live; daughter,
many still flock around Apostasy; am I to
remain silent? today again I descend in My
saving help and in the middle of their
rebellion I cry out: "Salvation! Salvation
comes from Me!" the earth is pining away
in its apostasy, consumed in its iniquity, and
its inhabitants are paying the penalty of its
sins; famines, earthquakes and wars; what-

28

ever comes out of the earth returns back to
earth .... cross, daughter, with Me this desert;
I Am is with you; stay cheerful and in
peace for I am with you;

Have You something to tell (.....) Lord?
for him? tell him: it is by faith that
I led you into My redemptive plans and it
will be by faith you will continue: I have
put you to the test and I tell you: I
know your activities, your love and the child-
like-faith; nevertheless, I have one complaint:
I have given you strength and perseverance

29

to help you (...)* yet how I wish you would consume it entirely! I have opened My Mouth and I have spoken; come, if you love listening you will learn; I, Yahweh, give you the Seal of My Eternal Love ♡ I Am is with you;

A ⳩ Ω

26. 5. 94

peace be with you; say these words to Me:

My Jesus You are my only Love in my heart,

my only Hope in my life,

* God was delicate not to write a few words, for exposing this person.

30

my only light in my soul,
for this reason remain with me Christ;
my guilt is overwhelming me,
and I am sorry for having sinned,
come and free me from all my sins,
do not prolong Your silence,
come and renew me,
stir me with Your Wisdom
and let Your Holy Spirit be my Ruler;
Amen ♡

say it now to ♡Me with confidence; I
am standing before you, My Hand on you;

31

I felt pity for you; keep My Rules securely
in your heart and do not shudder
when you see Me coming to you with My
bow and arrows, My arm still has to
shatter a few more rocks inside you;
come and write with your Saviour; do
not fear; it is I, Jesus Christ, your
Wealth ♡ ic

27. 5. 94

lean on Me, daughter; do not allow the
dead* to draw you back to them; have

* Spiritually dead : meaning, the world should not
tempt me and I should stay away from
temptation

32

you eaten from My fruit?

Yes I have eaten Your Words and they
are Life.

and you have revived; I am the Resurrection[*]; you have resurrected[*]; learn how
My Spirit works; My Spirit was deeply
moved to see you lying dead among the
dead; together with others, you had plunged
yourself to the bottom of the grave,
in the darkness, in the depths of

[*] The Lord is talking about the first resurrection,
the one of the spirit by the Holy Spirit.

33

putrefaction *¹; part - of - My - Body , My City,
you had ears but heard nothing ; you
had eyes but saw nothing ; weighed
down by your sins , you were choking
in the dust among dust *²; yet not one
of you were born there ; and I , seeing you
in this misery , was filled with sorrow;
My Eyes were worn out with suffering ;
I called to you all day , but not
one of you listened to the sound of My

* ¹ I remembered just before my conversion I saw a
vision of a leper . The leper was me.
* Jesus means the spiritually dead.

34

pleading; to honour My Name and to
honour the Hands that created you and
held you firm, and for the sake of My
Faithful Love, I revealed My Face to you
and shone on you My Light; Sovereignty
stood facing you, and ever so generously
My Holy Spirit breathed on you the
Breath of Life, the Breath of Resurrection ♡ the Word then anointed you
and ♡ His Royal Throne He established
in you; and to honour His Crown

35

in the dust*, He raised you from dust
triumphing in you, becoming the flower of
His Strength ; you see, daughter, My Love
works wonders for the dead .... then, I
spoke in My sanctuary², I split it open and
marched with glory in My domain ; I was
the One who fortified you, city, so that
Deception and Trickery would be unable to
lead their armies against you ♡ since you
have been raised up to walk with a King*³

---

* ...." in the dust", expression from our Lord which
means " in you", since we are made out of dust.
² It means: God spoke inside me.
³ Himself.

36

in His triumphal procession; and now
that I have resurrected you, you must give
up entirely all that the world offers you;
now that I resurrected you, do not look
to your left nor to your right but only
to the things above; let your thoughts be
heavenly thoughts; aspire from Me and not
from the dust; in your resurrection I
have stripped you off from your worldly
vestments and adorned your soul now
with My impressive Vestments; yes, I have
clothed you with Wisdom .... and the

37

Image of the unseen God is now reflected on you to lead you into divinity; I have asked the Father to vest you with <u>Myself</u> so that I lead you into sanctification; free at last ! .... and in this image I will draw My people into unity; be gentle and patient until the second resurrection; you received the Spirit of adoption through grace, this is why your lips are able to cry out: "Abba", a grace enough to lead you to heaven; continue with zeal and confidence since I am your Holy

38

Companion, and even if you are hounded, endure it passively; I will progressively lift the veil covering your spirit so that you may be revealed with Me in the fulness of My Glory; I Am is with you; praise the Amen and live for Me; this was a brief reminder to remind you where I had found you ♡   ΙΧΘΥΣ ⊂⊃•

30. 5. 94

Yahweh, my Good Father,
my soul yearns to live in Your House,
O listen to my appeal!
You who freed me to set me at Large
to display Your Holy Name

39

to multiple nations and extol
You with praises, tell me, my Good
Father, tell me, when will I hide
in the shadow of Your Wings?
    Have pity on me the sinner,
for I am a constant wretch, but by Your
    saving power, I know and I
    believe, You can lift me up.
I promise that ever hopeful I will
    honour Your Name more and more,
and my lips shall speak of Your
marvels.
        O Father, as the heavens and
earth acclaim You,
        for myself, come,
    in Your loving kindness, come,
    in Your great tenderness, come;
come and make us one, Yahweh.
    Yahweh, why do You wait so long?
Come now and heal our broken hearts.

daughter, I love you; I will make you all

40

one; see? and I will assemble you from far and wide and from every roadway, at the favourable time I will call; come near Me My child* and listen to this.: from the beginning I have been watching you; I have been speaking, but the passions of the world are increasing and the guilt of this generation will come crashing down when I will come and purge the nations, then they will lift their heads and will look for My Spirit that will lead

* Here, Yahweh sounded very much like a tender father.

4

them into the full knowledge of the truth;
this is why, daughter, you must intercede
for the East and the West to meet and
join their heart into one; this should be
done before the Enemy subdues My Law and
fertilizes My Sanctuary with human doctrines and
regulations; but it has been said that as
there were false prophets in the past history
among you, so you too will have your false
teachers, who will insinuate their own
disruptive views and disown the divinity
of My Son, Jesus Christ; these false

42

teachers intellectualize the Good News that
had been given to you in all their richness;
I tell you solemnly:

beware of the Deceiver, the Deceiver will
bring a different doctrine and will distort
My Word and the Tradition that were
passed on to you; so I am telling you,
do not imitate the deceiver; from all
that I have been writing to you, generation,
using My instrument's hand, heart and
soul, do not be afraid from these deceivers,
they are not gods and I am in every

43

faithful heart; I will unleash a torrential rain of fire on this earth to burn her crimes, but I will rescue My people ♡

- A ✗ Ω

31. 5. 94

My Lord?

I Am; Vassula of My Sacred Heart; rejoice and realize how out of a withered tree I made a fruitful tree, giving life by just one of My glances; so rejoice, daughter; I Am is with you; do not fear, My child, listen and write: every Easter season

44

I must drink from the cup of your
division since this cup is forced on Me;
but you too, daughter, will drink from it;
you shall share with Me what is bitter —
given by human hand; the more time
passes for them to unite the dates of Easter,
the more severe will be the sentence this
generation will receive; My Return is imminent and woe to the unrepentant
heart! woe to the divided heart! woe
to the unreconciled heart! 'they shall
be thrown down to hell!' (Mt : 11 : 23)

45

today every member of My House who pro-
vokes Me and enshrines the disastrous
abomination in his heart, will have his
name erased from the book of life for
having blasphemed; many of you, generation, listen to My Words but remain inactive in a spirit of lethargy; why do
you allow yourselves to be defeated and conquered by your incredulity? your apostasy
has coarsened your hearts and, Isaiah's
prophecy to this day stands and is being
fulfilled: ' you will listen and listen

46

again, but not understand, see and see again, but not perceive; for the heart of this nation has grown coarse, their ears are dull of hearing, and they have shut their eyes, for fear they should see with their eyes, hear with their ears, understand with their heart and be converted and be healed by Me *; repent! for the Kingdom of heaven is close at hand; look around you and see: one section of My Church has been blinded because of their nation-

* Is 6 : 9 - 10

47

alistic mind, a sluggish spirit settled upon
them; today I am speaking through the
mouths of Nothingness to show My Infinite
Mercy to all mankind but only one hand-
ful can hear and see Me; the rest were
not allowed to hear or see the Holy Spirit
of Truth *; but, like those who heard My
Spirit of Grace, they too are loved by
Me and this is why to this day I am
holding back My Father's Hand from falling

* I was wondering why and as if the Lord wanted
to stop me from thinking wrong, He hurried up and
said what followed.

48

upon them; no, daughter, they were not allowed to hear or see the splendour of the Truth and never will, not until their mind be renewed by a spiritual revolution; so long as they follow their course intellectually they will remain in the dark and estranged to My signs and marvels; so long as they make recourse to their own spirit they will continue to cross-examine My Holy Spirit of Truth without recognizing Him, He who is speaking now to them; with unseeing eyes and inattentive

49

ears, they will continue to proclaim their laws instead of My Law; they will try to change seasons and words, and because of their infidelity they will cancel My Traditions to human analogies, without the Truth that is in Me; they will boast of their achievement but it will only be acclaimed and praised by the corrupted world not by My Own whom I have sealed; yes,* the people of the world will rejoice and will celebrate this event even to ex-

* Ap. 11 : 10

50

change gifts between them ; but My Own will shed tears of sorrow and will wear sackcloth lamenting that this iniquity, this abomination of the desolation will not last forever ; Moses wrote : " those who keep the Law will draw life from it ; " and today I tell you : " <u>those who keep My Traditions will draw life from Them ;</u> " and when you confess that I, Jesus, am Lord, raised from the dead, then you <u>shall</u> be saved ; when with all your heart you will say My Words of

51

Institution on the Eucharist and Consecration, you will be saved! this is why in My Infinite Love I am calling you all to stretch out your hands for heavenly things only; ask for My Spirit to guide you and you will be in no danger of yielding to temptation; allow yourselves to be directed by My Spirit and no temptations can touch your spirit ... so you read how it was written that My Church would suffer and be under persecution, under the law of the Unlawful One, <u>betrayed from within,</u>

52

you will now be witnesses to this and all visions will come true;

Why had all this to come, Lord?

alas! many of your shepherds are asleep, and My lambs are scattered with so very few to rally them;

Lord, is it because some of Your shepherds scorn Your warnings? Is it because they take everything as a menace?

it is because I expose their nakedness; My Eyes are too pure to rest on sin and apathy and I cannot endure iniquity anymore; hear Me: their incredulity on

53

My Holy Spirit's gifts is standing in My way! if they only knew what I, God, am offering them, they would have been the ones to ask for more prodigies; now, have you not heard: " the amount you measure out is the amount you will be given and more besides; for the man who has will be given more; from the man who has not, even what he has will be taken away!"*¹ the lure of riches*²

*¹ Mk 4:24-25
*² It means 'pride'. Spiritual pride.

54

came inside these people and choked My
Word *, and so they produce nothing;
therefore, My Kingdom shall be taken
away from them and will be given to a
people who could produce its fruit; I, Jesus
bless you, daughter, have My Peace and
caress Me with your love; ic

2. 6. 94

Lord, my God, You who rejoice to give
Your gifts in secret, I ask You so much to

---

* I understood that although they study the Scriptures they do not penetrate in the meaning of the
Word and understand it with their own human light
and not with the Divine Light of the Holy Spirit.

55

give to all souls the greatest gift : the
  gift that transfigures our stained image
into the brightness of Your Divine Image.
  Turn us into Your reflection so that we
penetrate into Your Divinity.   Just as in
  the Day of Your Transfiguration, let
this become for us a second new feast of
  transfiguration so that we too may
hear those words from the Father: "These
are my sons and daughters, the beloved;
  they enjoy My favour, listen to them."
Then let us go out, with Your Spirit of Truth
  to tell of Your mighty deeds. Let it be
the Transfiguration of all the world *;
and in our transfiguration we will learn
  to love, and love will lead us to eternal
  life.

you have said well, daughter; ask for
this gift in your daily prayers and I

* Allusion to Ap. 21

56

shall give it to you; see how My garments are spattered in blood? see how My garments are red, soaked in My Blood? many unclean things render Me in this pitiable state .... many indeed are My groans and My Heart is lacerated by the very hands I have formed .... but so few listen to My groans, so few pay attention to My Tears of Blood; My Eyes waste away with weeping; I allow My images to weep to awaken your remorse and your pain but what I hear is a short sigh

57

in which I find a brief relief from it then,
but so very quickly you grant your heart
to be taken away by the worries of the
world; you allow your heart to be
taken away from comforting Me and being
a consoler to the Consoler, He who could
transfigure you, who could resurrect your
soul, who could divinize your soul ...
others, upon seeing the torrents shed from
My Eyes remain untouched because of their
incredulity; having lost the sense of My
wonders, they fail to understand and

58

with frenzy persecute My signs ; their sins
have 'choked' their heart and from thereon
their heart flutters after worldly things,
never realizing how their soul is being
misled by the evil one; who could possibly
understand My deep grief ?   why do they
give My Enemy cause to gloat over them in
secret ? who of you could give Me relief ?
who of you can give Me rest ? every
hour that a day contains, every minute
that exists I am near you and call to
you: " return to Me, return to Love ; "

59

oh, but so many of you have grown cruel.....
you see Me soaked in My Blood, yet you
grant your eyes to rest; oh .... until
when will you not hear your God wailing?

.... as for you, flower, remember the
affection I have for you and My love;

abandon yourself to Me; come and comfort
Me with your love; let the nations re-
discover Me through you,* demonstrate My
love, My sorrow and My anguish I
have for them; living tablet! I, Jesus

* When I witness about Him.

60

Christ have entrusted you with My Message, do not doubt .... I have given you a Treasure into your hands, I have given you My entire Heart into your hands, what more could I have given you? since it is through My generosity I have raised you to enter this state of grace in which I keep you, tolerate your adversaries with love; have you not heard that sufferings bring patience? I tell you, they bring you closer to Me; I have poured into your heart through My Holy Spirit My

61

intense Knowledge, a royal vestment, to
be worn for My glory; I have appointed
you to glorify Me; all that I have
given you pleases Me and the Father; I
delight to make you the delight of My Eyes,
the joy of My Heart; in your simplicity
My Soul rejoices! so do not refuse Me
anything; instruct the unlearned and do
not allow the evil one to rob the hours I
want with you; *— instruction will lead
many to become the delight of My Soul; in

* In dictation.

62

the end Our Two Hearts will defeat the
Enemy and that transfiguration you have
asked for will take place : I shall
renew the face of this earth ♡ I,
Jesus bless you ; ic

3. 6. 94

My Lord ?

I Am ; little one My Peace I give to you ;
daughter, many people come to you and ask :
"is all well ? what has Jesus to tell us these days ?"
daughter from Egypt, this is what you
should say to these people : ´ Jesus

63

tells you, generation, that you have still not recovered from your illness, you certainly have not recovered from your apostasy* and there is more than a beam in your eye; generation, to this day, Love is rejected, yet in My Mercy, I wait patiently for the tribute you owe Me, your God. I wait patiently for all of you to attain the full measure of your sins before My Justice falls over you; let Me put it to you this way: return to Me and repent from your heart, change this desert

* The general Apostasy around the world.

64

that you have become, into a garden, into an Eden, <u>love</u>! love one another! live the Gospel and do not cross-examine one another; look at your own beam first in your eye, pray without ceasing, live holy; do not allow your eyes to rest; reconcile with your brothers*[1] and you will escape death; do not persecute all that is holy; confess sincerely and with your entire being*[2], do not delude yourself;*[3] the

---

*[1] Term that means with everyone.
*[2] Meaning also to mortify your body, by fasting.
*[3] It means, it is not enough to just go to confess for the sake of confessing, one must really <u>feel</u> the sins and be sincere while confessing.

Excerpts from Notebook 72

**NB
72**

7 June 94, NB p.5 (Greece—Blessed Mother) . . . Message For Rhodes Prayer Group
✠ My mantle covers Jesus' little flock

10 June 94, NB p.7 (Fairfield, Ct.) . . . My Delight Is In Every Pure Heart
✠ My joy is when I see your eyes seeking only Heavenly things
✠ My Splendour is when you keep My sanctuary holy

11 June 94, NB p.10 (So. Hadley) . . . Love: Disarm The Enemy, Defeat The Divider
✠ I shall fill their mouths with My spiritual food

13 June 94, NB p.15 (Gaithersburg) . . . Rest Now, My Child

14 June 94, NB p.16 (So. Carolina) . . . My Presence Should Satisfy You

15 June 94, NB p.16 (Notre Dame) . . . You Allow Me To Efface You
✠ I...give your society memories of My Holy Countenance

17 June 94, NB p.18 . . . All That I Have To Say Will Be Said
✠ I just need your will and your consent to complete My Work

18 June 94, NB p.20 (Stockton, CA) . . . Return To Me And You Will Live Forever
✠ I shall speak with authority through your mouth
✠ Come and make peace with Me, your God

19 June 94, NB p.24, Fathers' Day (San Francisco) . . . I Am Their First Father
✠ Bring back My children to Me...I am their Holy Companion

20 June 94, NB p.28 (Toronto) . . . I Am Your Best Friend
✠ My Teachings will open a broad highway

21 June 94, NB p.31 (Toronto) . . . Your Eyes Will See My Sovereignty
✠ Salvation is at hand's reach

22 June 94, NB p.32 . . . Look! I Have Spread My Message In Every Nation

24 June 94, NB p.34 (Ottawa) . . . Very Soon, God Will Be Coming To Live Among You
✠ If you wish, you can be taught through My Own Lips!

26 June 94, NB p.36 (Ottawa) . . . My Thirst For Wretched Souls Is Great
✠ One day I will show you the vast multitude of souls I saved through the wounds your detractors imposed on you

29 June 94, NB p.39 . . . Guard All That I Have Given You
✠ In your submissiveness you inherit My Will

2 July 94, NB p.41 . . . Your Work Is Not In Vain
✠ I know how much a household requires from the mistress of the house...I am with you at all times

4 July 94, NB p.43 . . . I Have Put My Angels In Charge Of My Messages
✠ I shall raise disciples, form them and set them off to witness on My Message
✠ My Message Saves; this is why Satan, knowing how many souls would escape him, pursues his battle

10 July 94, NB p.51 . . . You Will Turn Into A Copy Of Myself
✠ Your abode is in Us, the Most Holy Trinity

17 July 94, NB p.53 (Greece—Simi) . . . No Evil Can Become Heir To My Kingdom
Message of Saint Michael
✠ My eyes are worn out with vexation and the violence of the world
✠ Who among you delights in Life? Then come closer to the Holy One and never give up

19 July 94, NB p.60 (Rhodes) . . . Be Eager To Receive My Word; It Is Your Nourishment

TRUE LIFE IN GOD

Creator tells you: despise all that is unholy, observe heaven and be witnesses of the Most High; give yourselves more to prayer and beg your Creator to be your Light and your Guide; return to Me so that I may wash clean the sins you commit night and day; your illness is not incurable, although your guilt and your so many sins are like bitter plague on your soul, I can heal your guilt, I can forgive you and restore your whole body... anyone who loves his life loses it;

2

anyone who loses his life in this world
will keep it for the eternal life; many of
you read My Messages but fail to understand
the Heart of the Message, because you are
not well rooted in Me; you follow the
letter of these Messages but fail to penetrate
in the core of the Message! I tell you
solemnly, freedom is to be found in a
rebirth from the Spirit, only then, when
the Spirit opens your eyes will you know
the Greatness of My Name and the depths
of My Sublime Glory; surely you know

3

that you harvest what you reap; if you
sow in a field of dissension you will get
a harvest of feuds and rivalry; if you
sow in a field of accusations you will get
a harvest of self-condemnation; if you
sow in a field of calumny you will get a
harvest of your own downfall out of it;
sow the seeds of love in your field and
you will harvest a return of love; sow in
a field of forgiveness you will get a
harvest of mercy; do not self-appoint
yourselves as judges, I am the Sole Judge ....

4

as before I am telling you : I do not come
to condemn the world since I am here to
save the world; I am here now to warn the
world, so you who condemn so quickly and
who crowned yourself as judge, I tell you:
you have your judge already! tell those
who ask you, daughter, if all is well,
to stay awake, praying at all times for
the strength to survive all that is
going to happen; that will do, daughter
stand by Me faithfully and be in constant
prayer; My child, I, Jesus, will help you

5

in this extensive journey you will undertake for My sake*; I, Jesus bless you and fr. Michael; Love is near you; ic

7. 6. 94

Our Blessed Mother gives a message to the prayer group of Rhodos, Greece.

have My Peace; I already said: I will return to them on Thursday in a special way, this is the way; I wish to tell them these words: you want to be perfect in beauty? gather as you do and pray together with Me, I say 'together with Me' because

---

* Several meetings in the USA and Canada + TV programs.

6

while you are praying, I too am praying with you, My children; oh how your prayers console Me .... do not be afraid of human opposition, this has to come, but you have your arbitrator; it is I; uncovered you are not; My mantle covers Jesus' little flock; be faithful to Jesus and to Me, group of Our Hearts; the wicked will have no power over you, My little ones; remain awake and watchful in prayer; We bless you all, daughters and sons of the Most High ♡

TRUE LIFE IN GOD

7

U.S.A. - Fairfield Ct. 10. 6. 94

Lord ? I'm at Your service.

I Am; here I am, by your side I stand; put your hope in Me and securely you will stand; oh daughter, tell them, tell them that My Heart is an abyss of Love and Mercy; the Spirit whom I am sending you will remind you of the Truth and that I Am; listen and write: peace be with you; little children, My delight is in every pure heart, My joy is when I see your eyes seeking only heavenly things; My glory is

8

when you come to Me and tell Me: " here
I am .... here I am ," offering your heart to
Me to transfigure it into My domain and then
reign over it ; My magnificence and My
splendour are when you keep My sanctuary*
holy, turning it into a glorious domain
for My majesty ; My sovereignty is when in
your wretchedness and in your poverty you
can cry out :" hosanna! hosanna! to
the King who saved us, for eternity !"
.... this is My Glory .... by your sacrifice

* our soul

9

I make gardens out of deserts .... by your love, I raise up the dead*; by your thirst for Me your God, you console Me and become a comforting balm for My wounded Heart .... lift up your eyes, child, and look at the One who leans from above to lift you to Him ; come, cities of Mine and join in one voice and in one heart the prayer I have taught you to say :

(pray.)

I bless you from the core of My Sacred

* Spiritually dead.

10

Heart; I bless you leaving the Sigh of My
Love on your forehead ♡ be one

ΙΧΘΥΣ 🐟

South Hadley, MA. 11. 6. 94

My Lord?

I Am; have My Peace, hear My Voice:
daughter, I will infuse in you My Spirit
and you shall open your mouth this
evening and My Words will pour out like
manna feeding a multitude; I shall fill
their mouths with My spiritual food and
once filled they shall praise Me and glorify
Me: tell them that the One who sits

11

on a glorious throne calls out for peace, reconciliation and love; you want to extol My Name? then rise and go now and reconcile with your brothers, with your sisters; never would you be so near My Heart than in this moment of reconciliation .... disarm the enemy, defeat the divider for the rest of your days .... come, what I ask from you is love, and I shall frown on you no more; blessed one*, every minute you give Me pleases Me, so I, Jesus, will preserve you

* Jesus turned to me to speak to me

12

from becoming elated; ...* do not deny now that you would rather rest than have My dic-tation *² ....

It is true;' I am very tired.

just one word: Vassula, I desire to keep you in My Heart forever, so love Me ....

Are You upset now Lord? *³

no; I know how strained you are and your limits of strength; all I ask is love from

---

* Suddenly Jesus stopped and asked me the following very earnestly.
*² I was so tired and He knew it.
*³ Though He did not appear upset.

13

you; have Me in your mind; your heart, and your sight, so that you accomplish with Me this work with a triumphant crown; delight Me and lean on Me; I raised you to glorify Me; I raised you so that I may say one day: " look! this is the one I selected to glorify Me with her love; this is the one I have espoused, My bride and My beloved, and on whom I have given My traits to testify for love. this is the one whom My Holy Spirit endowed with Wisdom, anointing her with

TRUE LIFE IN GOD

14

My Signature*, ah! how I delight to have raised her, for now I can acclaim that no one in her generation loved Me as much as she has ♡ My desire has been fulfilled My teachings were not in vain; I have done what I have done to honour My Name;" around you, My child, I Am is always with you; you are never alone and My Heart leaps with joy every time you utter My Name to glorify Me": let it be known

* That is when He appears in public in my place.

15

that the Holy One is in command of everything and that I am an abyss of Mercy ♡ I love you;　be in peace: ic

Gaithersberg, MD. 13. 6. 94

Very late at night after the conference. I was very tired but I went to Christ.

Lord?

I Am; little one have My Peace; I tell you, you have no idea how happy you make Me coming at this hour seeking Me; I tell you, My Heart rejoices, My Vassula; I bless you from the core of My Heart; rest

16

now My child; Jesus is My Name and I
am near you; IΧΘΥΣ ⤳🐟

Greensville S. Carolina   14. 6. 94

Jesus reassures me before the meeting.

lean on Me entirely; lift your head and
look at Me: never forget that I am always
with you; My Presence should satisfy you; I
Jesus bless you; ic

South Bend – Notre Dame   15. 6. 94

Lord?

I Am; little one feel My Presence; I am the
Rock of your salvation; allow Me to expand
My dynasty, call and I shall answer you;

17

Lord, why do You appear in my place so often now?

I had been saying: to you I shall offer My Song and to prove My faithful Love I would give your society memories of My Holy Countenance .... since it is My Own Love Hymn to you all; and you daughter, My Harp, I allow My Light to cover you; since you allow Me to efface you, My wonder takes place; this is My gift to you; precious it is and you did not merit it, but it pleased the Father to give it to you for within

18

it is His Seal; you allowed Us*¹, daughter, to lay Our Hands upon you, you allow Us still to dwell in you, Vassula, for no one has the Father done this*²; no other has known this gift, a gift given to all of you through His Love Hymn ♡ come, We*³ are with you; Our blessings are upon you ♡

A ☧ Ω

17.6.94

O Come Lord, come and transfigure our wretchedness into Your Perfect Image. We are so

* The Holy Trinity spoke   *² Jesus spoke.
*³ The Holy Trinity spoke again.

19

far from what You call perfect! How are we
ever going to join You into Your Kingdom with
what we are now? I miss You very much....

have My Peace; I am the Vine and you are
part of Me; allow Me to nourish you with
My sap and you will live! I have instructed
you with Wisdom to bear fruit in holiness;
remain, daughter, in Me; do not be astonished anymore*; remember, all that I have
to say will be said: all the people who will
have to hear will hear; I enjoy sharing My

---

* My mind 'reels' now and then how His Messages took
such amplitude in a short period and all He has given me.

20

plans with you; this Work is not yours but
Mine; I just need your will and your consent
to complete My Work; are you still willing
to remain the instrument of My desires?

Yes, Lord, You know I want to remain with You.

I bless you, daughter, I love you; My Heart
rejoices to hear your consent, not that I
doubted, but it pleases Me to <u>hear</u> from
the one I have raised, these words ♡ ic

Stockton, CA.- U.S.A.   18. 6. 94
- Before the meeting in the Cathedral.
My Lord?

21

I Am;* lean on Me; this is My assembly;
it is I who opened the doors for you to
glorify My Name; so do not worry about
what you will say; My Spirit will be
upon you; I shall speak with authority through
your mouth, yes; you shall be My Echo!
and I will pour My treasures on this wretched
generation to enrich their spirit with My
Spirit; I will fill their mouths with My
Celestial Manna; I will, Myself, give them
prosperity and their soul will yield a divine
harvest since the seeds will descend from

* The Father answered.

22

Divinity; will I not give them life again to rejoice in Me? will I not grant them, as a tender Father, My saving help? in their poverty I, Myself, shall guard them for I am faithful .... and I will raise them in their poverty to praise and hallow My Name; I am a God full of pity and My Heart can be touched; come and learn:

- in the morning sow your seed of love;
- at noon sow your seed of peace;
- in the evening sow your seed of reconciliation; then go and collect your harvest and

23

offer it to Me, your Father in Heaven, and
I will tell you:

" in your graciousness, My child, you
have obtained your reward in heaven; "
from above I call to you all:

" come! come and make peace with Me,
your God and you will have My Blessings;
return to Me and you will live forever;

A ☧ Ω

24

Father's Day.   San Francisco   19. 6. 94

Yahweh, Creator and Father of all, I love You. There is certainly no Father like You.

Father, I admit that we are hard in the heart and, ah, so distant from Your Loving Heart .... We cannot say that we have not heard about the greatness of Your Love, yet our ears have not been attentive and we have ignored You .... We have rebelled against You...

Father, we are filled with misery and we are champions when it comes to wickedness. The whispering of our hearts are venomous and our soul is as night.

O Father, I admit that we have turned Your House into the haunt of the lizard and the spider, yet, Your right Hand was not hidden, You had filled us with good things!

Father, in our immense pride, we have betrayed Your Image, we have committed a double

25

crime : disloyalty and division . We fail to give water to the thirsty , we fail to give bread to the hungry ; spite is our daily bread thus provoking the pillars of heaven to tremble ....
We have all become like withered leaves because of our division ; can we say : " We have been invoking Your Name in one voice ? "

Yet, Father, Your lips, wet with graciousness, never cease from calling us with blessings. Your Eyes are drawn to Your creatures with pity ; your majesty visits the earth planting vineyard after vineyard , how blessed those whom You visit, and invite to walk with You in Your celestial courts !

Father, our faults overwhelm us and our hearts are gross with sin , yet in Your Mercy You blot every evil out .

Is there anyone today who remembers You ?
Is there anyone offering You a thought ?
Is there anyone comforting You ?

26

daughter? have My Peace; - look, I do not condemn anyone, flower; hear Me: <u>bring back My children to Me</u>; appease My indignation against them! offer Me this as a gift on Father's day; remind them daughter, as you have done today that I am their first Father, their comrade and best friend, the Upright One who watches them and loves them; I am their Holy Companion; tell My children to whom they should bound themselves by intimate friendship and how to put their trust in Me; - hear Me:

27

for My sake be constant in your prayers,
you are bound by the vows you so generously made, vows of faithfulness to your
Father; I am Yahweh and you are bound
to Me with bonds of love; ah daughter
satisfy your Father's thirst for his children
by loyally offering yourself as a sacrifice;
allow Me to use you to speak in their
heart and stir their love. My sighing is
no secret from you; your Father's sighing
is no secret from you; My child; be
gentle in carrying out My Message, I

28

Am is always with you; do not be afraid,
the more you advance, the more you
should lower yourself, take courage, I will
renew you all in the end in My Love;

A ☧ Ω

— Before the meeting — Toronto —   20. 6. 94

Lord?

I Am; be in peace; I Jesus love you, always
remember this;

Lord; direct my steps as You have promised
me; I am ready to go and serve You,
Your Majesty. Let Your word be in my
mouth; You are the joy of my heart;
away from me I am nothing and am

29

paralyzed; wholeheartedly I now entreat You to help me.

blessed of My Soul what would I not do for you.... so be it, My little companion, My Spirit will be upon you, not only because you have asked, but because My Name will be glorified through your mouth; My Teachings will open a broad highway so that many will be able to walk in it; I am your best Friend and I shall help you always; ΙΧΘΥΣ ⊃⟩○

30

— Toronto —   21. 6. 94

My Lord and my Shepherd, in Your kindness
multiply Your noble vineyards, let there
be more workers in them to proclaim
Your Royal Authority, then, every nation
will see Your 'Glory'!

peace My child; when these heavens will
be rolled up like a scroll* and the earth
will wear away, they will see My Glory;
all of those remaining will gaze on your
King; your eyes will see My Sovereignty;
I shall not cease calling to My children
until I restore Jerusalem ♡

                                    ΙΧΘΥΣ 🐟

* as in my vision.

31

21. 6. 94

Lord ?

I Am; peace My child, Yahweh is with you, and I bless you; have Me locked in your heart — come My child, your race is not over and although your Abba is sometimes testing you*, you are never alone; be patient and I will continue to instruct you and give you My directives for I am determined to revive My children and bring them out of their lethargy; I will take their atrophy in consideration and I

* By not feeling His Presence.

32

will be charitable to them ; the Amen is
at your very doors ; Salvation is at
hand's reach ; come ;

A ☧ Ω

22. 6. 94

My God ?

I Am ; peace be with you ; know that
what I have given you as task is beyond
your normal strength , but do not forget
that I am your Strength ; without Me
you would never manage ... look ! I have
spread My Message in every nation ; I gave

33

an order in heaven and My word flashed on earth; tell Me, at whose command were you raised up? and who withstood the might of My command? I have raised you to be My witness and through your mouth heal the broken hearts, raise the dead and be a menace to My enemy; on you I will continue to engrave with My Finger My Love Hymn; come;

ΙΧΘΥΣ <°)))))><

34

— Congress in Ottawa   24.6.94
(Before speaking to the youngsters: message
that was read out to them.)

O Lord, my Life, my Joy, my Smile, my
Plenitude, my Rock, my Salvation, my
Sweet Torment, let Your arrows fly on
Your Target; in the path You prescribed
for me, I find Your Presence, the Reward of
Your arrows, and, on walking You fill
my soul with living waters, so, what more
could I ask?

display then My marvels and My kindness to this wretched generation; I am
glorified every time you pronounce My Name
with love; I love you My pupil; tell.
them* to allow Me to become their

* The youngsters.

35

personal Teacher, their welfare, their guide,
their counsellor and mostly their Holy
Companion; My Law is a Law of Love
My Law is a Law of Hope, but the
evil one contradicts the Truth; if
you wish, My child, you can be taught
through My Own Lips! do not be
ashamed to confess your sins, My good
pleasure is to forgive you; I shall show
My sweetness towards your weakness
because My Love for you is Infinite;
I tell you: soon, very soon, God

36

will indeed be coming to live among you;
I bless each one of you leaving the
Sign of My Love on your forehead;

A ☧ Ω

Ottawa 26. 6; 94

My Lord?
I Am .... why are you dwindling away
like a shadow?

It looks like I have become an object of
derision ... I know when someone avoids me;
how many more malicious things will they
say about me? even in return for my
friendship, they denounce me, though
all I had done was Your Will : I pray for
them, sacrifice for them. Will You not
defend my innocence?

37

do not fear for I am near you; allow
these things to happen for with this
sacrifice I obtain souls who are on the
road to perdition; ah Vassula .... one
day I will show you the vast multitude
of souls I saved through the wounds
your detractors imposed on you and
through your acts of reparation....
My Love for souls passes every possible
understanding and I tell you, My thirst
for wretched souls is great! how can
I then remain indifferent, My Vassula?

38

how? when hordes of nations fall into apostasy and rebellion? today's rebellion is even greater than the Great Rebellion known in the past;* does a shepherd abandon his flock.? I am your Shepherd and I love My little flock; now, I and you will continue to work together; your work is not in vain and My Heart delights every time your lips pronounce My Name; every fibre of My Heart loves you .... come, lean on Me and satisfy

* Allusion to Ps 95

39

My thirst by bringing Me souls, and I shall continue to send you in every nation to proclaim My Love Hymn; and upon you, My myrrh, My shadow will confirm the reality of My Presence, because My signs will accompany you ♡ come now;

A☧Ω

Ottawa 29. 6. 94

You are my Salvation.

I am your Salvation, child! and you, you are My adopted one! so lean on Me! – in your weakness you inherit My Strength

40

‑ in your submissiveness you inherit My Will;

‑ in your total effacement you become heiress of My Image;

‑ in your poverty you inherit what the sages are looking for but never can inherit it¹, you inherit My Wisdom;

do not substitute your gifts for anything in this world, guard them preciously till I come to fetch you, as a spouse who lifts his bride over the threshold, I, too in that hour, I will lift you, My beloved, to enter My Glory .... therefore, guard

41

preciously all that I have given you and do not listen to your wrong - doers, My precious one ..... Prisoner - of - My - Love, yet never more free, are you happy to be with Me in this way?

I am unworthy - what can I reply? You know Lord, You know how happy I am.

come, we, us?

yes! always, we us.

2. 7. 94

Lord, Companion and God of my life, I have to observe today some house - duties.

42

I know, I know how much you have to do and how much a household requires from the mistress of the house, and I am pleased and glad you do the work;

I am with you at all times, My daughter, and I tell you: your work* is not in vain; My 'thorns' will be removed one after the other, for in you I shall raise disciples to glorify My Name; many of My Own betray Me and there is already now a division in

* The Lord means the household work but also His Work, I am doing, too.

43

My House .... all I ask from you is to lend Me your ear now and then during the day; you are My incense, come; ic

4. 7. 94

My Vassula ♡ in your days, your testimony will be reinforced by My Spirit; I will look after My Message so that My Words will find a home in each one of you; I tell you solemnly: testify in My Name and do not fear, I am with you; I shall raise disciples, form

44

them, then set them off to witness on
My Message; My Message saves; this is
why, Satan knowing how many souls
would escape him, will pursue his battle
on strayed souls and use them to falsify your life and the way you live,
by their lying pen! but they shall be
caught out, child! the more they
persecute you all the more I will encourage you and My people by showing Myself to them in your place: you are
My Echo, the Echo of the most Beloved

45

of the Father; this, as I have told you, My Vassula, is a gift from the Most High, so as to encourage you, and at the same time a seal of My Message ♡ the Father and I will look after you, My child, and I tell this generation what I had once said to My disciples : happy the eyes that see what they see,* for there are many who desire to see what they see and have not seen it ....

_____

* Those who have seen Him manifest Himself in the meetings.

46

so consider the privilege of you who saw
Me and rejoice! and you, daughter, allow
Me to efface you entirely to glorify My
Name; I have put My angels in charge
of My Messages to spread them far and
wide for I intend to govern the world
in holiness and purity ♡ persevere in your
mission and I tell you, My Heart
rejoices when I see you taking pleasure in
doing it! do not be affected by
your critics, lean on Me; ___
ah! will I rejoice when I see the

47

beginning of an analogy written on My
Message "! 'blessed is he who will serve
Me and esteems My Words of today ; I
will assist him ♡ ' tell *(....) that I take
in account all that he does ; ' My son,
do not take on a great amount of other
duties *²; they will only multiply and you
will suffer for lack of time '! hurry as
fast as you can, yet you will never arrive
if you ask Me ':" Lord, what are Your

---

* ' out of discretion the Lord allowed me to
avoid writing the name.
*² duties that distract him from True Life in God, (yes)

48

needs ? " I will tell you : " <u>My Message</u>
<u>saves</u>, and time is short, what you
have commenced I blessed ; give this generation My Bread of understanding to eat
and the water of wisdom to drink ;
My Message nourishes and quenches their
thirst ; this generation is dying fast for
lack of food ; the fruit of your labours*
will save many ; <u>hurry and consume</u>
now My Messages ; draw from them the
riches of My Sacred Heart ; then put these

* books on True Life in God. (yes!)

TRUE LIFE IN GOD

49

riches to light; I have given you health
to restore the health of My Church; draw
from My Messages all the light that is
required to enlighten the hearts of My
sacerdotal souls and the hearts of the laity;
I have given you a treasure of unity
within it, promote unity in the light of
My Message; quote My Words giving
parallels; hordes of nations will
be enlightened by the beauty of this
work; you have done well to write
about My Pope, but the Potter, out of

50

the same clay shaped My Patriarch Bartholomew*too; take as much pride in writing on your brother*, as you have written on My Pope! complete this work equally; I tell you, use My Messages, for within them you will be able to acquire enough knowledge to understand My desires; let your sole ambition from now on be to yield a rich harvest from True Life in God! I bless you and reassure you that My Mother

* Pat. Bartholomew

51

and I are united to you; ic

10. 7. 94

peace be with you; have as your daily
bread, prayers; let them fill your
mouth; I love hearing them; I am the
Breath of your life, say:

Lord of the Heavens,
sanctify my soul, Your dwelling place,
so that You, my King will be glorified;
crown my soul with holiness,
so that in Your Divinity I may become
heiress of Your Kingdom

52

and Your Glory;
I promise to lay down my life
for my brothers and my sisters,
and become part of Your Salvation Plan;
Creator, I am yours,
Jesus Christ, I am yours,
Holy Spirit, I am yours;
                              amen;
your abode is in Us, the Most Holy
Trinity; ecclesia will revive;

A ☧ Ω

53

daughter, love Me and you shall live;
eat Me and you will grow in Me;
drink Me and you will revive; if
you do these things you will turn into
a copy of Myself: your Divine God;
pupil, I love you and bless you;
Jesus is My Name: have My Peace ♡

ΙΧΘΥΣ 🐟

Greece - Simi island - Panormiti -   17. 7. 94
                  (- St. Michael's island).

Lord?

I Am; I can remain with you even in

54

your wretchedness; look, My daughter,
you have been assigned for this mission
to pronounce My Love Hymn and I, as
a harpist will play sweetly song after
song on you to make everyone remember Me;
tell all My children who heard My Love
Hymn that I, Yahweh, their Creator, am
their guardian; if you remain faithful
to Me, I will raise from Nothingness a
house in My Name; do not dread My
Ways and do not fear to approach Me;
I am your Father in heaven, so turn

55

your gaze upward and let your King
and Father of all, prepare in you an
everlasting sanctuary; My Eyes are worn
out with vexation and the violence of the
world, for no evil can become heir of
My Kingdom; observe My Commandments
and do not take them lightly; if you
follow them, they will keep you upright, even if you are utterly wretched
come to Me and tell Me:

"look Father, see all the stains on
my soul? I had no constancy in

56

Your Commandments, yet I know, Father, that You are all merciful and generous; from Your precepts I can learn Wisdom; teach me Your Will, Yahweh, teach me Your judgements; come and bind me to You, Father, and remind my wretched soul that I am heir of Your Kingdom too; though my temptations are count- less, I trust in Your Saving help; "

and I will answer you, My child: " blessed, ah blessed one of My Soul, at the memory of your creation, I wept;

57

I wept tears of joy ; I had set you in your mother's womb with a heart, to live and share My Glory ; do not turn away now ... I have heard your prayer that was said in purity of heart and I tell you : you are very precious in My Eyes, and now for the sake of My Love I have for you, seek from today :

love, peace and reconciliation − alone you are not ; I am with you always and bless you without ceasing ♡

Α☧Ω

58

(Same day, Saint Michael the Archangel
gave me this message:)

daughter of the Most High, allow Me to
tell God's children that they should
pursue Peace : " who among you delights in
life ? then come closer to the Holy One
and <u>never</u> give Him up .... stand <u>firm</u>
forever .... how blessed are those whose
God is Yahweh ! they are the heirs of
His Kingdom ! I tell you, friends of the
Christ, today Christ is wearing sackcloth to manifest His grief .... for the

59

sake of His Love, fast this Friday on bread
and water to relieve His Heart ; offer Christ
this sacrifice ; I have indeed called you
here to honour the Most High and I,
the archangel, Saint Michael, am
mightily touched by your visit ; My
hands are in full battle and My arm
is constantly raised to keep evil away ....
pray to Me as you do and encourage
others too to do the same ; the Enemy
of God weakens with this prayer* ;

* The small prayer to St. Michael (Pope Leon XIII)

60

praise God and no one else; lift your heads to God and to no one else; love God with all your heart and soul; do not fall into temptations; ponder on all the good things you receive from the Most High and bless Him; and now come and visit Me again*[1]; I love you;"

Saint Michael, God's Archangel;

-Rhodes- 19. 7. 94

Lord?

I Am; allow Me to be with you*[2];

*[1] In St. Michael's Church on the island.
*[2] In dictation.

61

set your heart right and behave according
to My Heart ; I am present;

I feel that I am far behind You in this
race and almost losing sight of You.
Am I an obstacle perhaps in Your divine
plan? am I slow? am I unfaithful?
am I giving honours on earthly things?

ah, you are weak, yet My Plan in you
will be accomplished because of your
thirst for Me; remain small so that
everyone around you may notice My Greatness.... do all you can and I will do
the rest;

Reassure me now from the Bible, please.

62

very well, then open the Bible*, yes, be eager to receive My Word; it is your nourishment and it keeps you alive; Vassula, My Heart bleeds when I see you sad .... feel My pain .... I want you to remain in My Peace and My Joy; do not fret and do not get upset on things that do not last! for My sake now, go to Saint George's Church and pray the rosary; I want you to set your hope on Me for I am rich in

* I did and I read.

63

happiness; generous too in giving it; amass all that is good from Me and fill your soul from Me who am the Source of your happiness; I possess the only true joy and life that lasts and is real; rely on My compassion and stop feeling guilty; I already have forgiven you; remember, although you have progressed you are still learning and you are still My pupil;

Not the best one though.

no; but I love you; I shall fortify you, pupil, so cling to Me, I Jesus;

64

will help you; ♡ ic

On the island of Patmos   22. 7. 94

Lord, rescue the weak and save the
wretched of this world.

peace be with you; grace is upon you;
daughter, My sighs from My Heart are
continuous; the humble, the wretched
and the innocent have heard Me and
they are the consolers of The Consoler;
Faithful - Love is among you all but not
everyone sees Me; I am putting all My
Heart into this* Love Hymn, I am putting
* True Life in God.

Excerpts from Notebook 73

22 July 94, continued from NB 72 p.64 (Patmos) . . . The Humble, The Wretched And The Innocent Have Heard Me
✠ I am putting all My Heart into this Love Hymn
✠ I will not stand by and watch this offspring of My Father take the shape of My enemy
✠ You are the offspring of the Most High
✠ The trumpet of the Sixth Angel will soon be heard

NB 73

23 July 94, NB p.7 (Patmos) . . . You Shall Suffer Too As He Suffered
✠ I will call and you should be aware of My call

29 July 94, NB p.10 . . . Spread In Every Nation The Fragrance Of The Knowledge Of Myself
✠ So will I produce spiritual food for the hungry and the poor

7 August 94, NB p.12 (Rhodes) . . . Pray For Your Priests
✠ Do not...be surprised that they mistrust the lot of you and argue on My Words...they are as dear to Me as you are...respect them and pray for them
✠ The Man of Peace will understand My Message
✠ Do not feed yourselves on things that are not holy
✠ If I, who love you, do not reprimand you, who will?

8 August 94, NB p. 18 . . . I Shall Bring Even Pagans To Desire Me
✠ ...I shall go to countries that never held My Name Holy
✠ I will continue to give you in secret the teachings of My Wisdom leaving the philosophers' mind in awe

10 August 94, NB p.26 . . . A Judge, Yet So Tender
✠ I am here to instruct the uninstructed and to give My Law to the lawless
✠ The bread that cures you comes from above
✠ Open your heart and you will receive light and you will believe

**18 August 94, NB p.32 (Blessed Mother) . . . This Special Grace...
Will Come To Its End**

✠ Every nation will read the Word of Life welcoming Christ

✠ Teach others to think of God...They will realize that God is Life, Joy and Heavenly Peace

✠ "How shall we possibly escape if we turn away from a voice that warns us from Heaven"...the retribution...is at hand

19 August 94, NB p.37 . . . Never Judge

✠ Learn the patience of the Father

23 August 94, NB p.41 . . . Daniel's Prophesy Will Be Fulfilled

✠ They shall officially declare that I should be abolished from within My Tabernacle

3 October 94, NB p.44 . . . Our Two Hearts Will Be Pierced

✠ Obey this shepherd no matter what happens

✠ Satan is on his way to My Throne

✠ By force and by treachery they will invade My House...The invader is a <u>scholar</u>...Many of you will lose faith

✠ I want you to be courageous...in the days of this great tribulation, continue to defend My Word

**5 October 94, NB p.56 . . . My Earnest Wish Is That The West and
East Meet**

✠ I need these two pillars to come together and consolidate My Church

✠ Any gathering in My Name for unity, My blessings are poured out

✠ Any step towards unity, all Heaven rejoices

✠ A traitor will bind My Law and My Tradition and subdue the pillar that honoured Me in the West

6 October 94, NB p.63 . . . My Love Is Infinite

all My Heart into hymns out of love for all of you, good or wicked; I have become a beggar for your sake, and if your God is limping by you and the passers-by do not recognize Me, it is because I am covered by blood and spittle from this generation living in iniquity and sin .... O earth, so defiled! you ceased to be .... your God has come to you but you have not re-cognized Him; have you not heard? I am Divine and in My Divinity I

2

I want to save you so that you too
may join the saints ; yet, despite My
offer many of My children do not want
to repent nor are they ready to give up
their sins, these sins that chain them to
everything but Me ; — My Soul is
full of sighs, yes, tell daughter, that
My sackcloth is soaked in My Blood ;
hear Me : today just as yesterday the
most Holy One is spat upon, scourged
by all passers by ; My Holy Cross, the
Instrument of your salvation is tread

3

upon by man daily ... ah ... I suffer grievously .... today I have opened My reserves in heaven to nourish you abundantly; I am making a road to lead you all to heaven ; I have said : " although this generation has thrust itself so willingly at Satan's feet , I, the Holy One, can never forget the memory of your creation and how at the memory of this instance My Father had shed tears of joy; this is why I will not stand by and watch this offspring of My Father take the

4

shape of My Enemy; the Enemy may have attraction but it is deadly, whereas what I have to offer will bring you to your divinity and back into your Father's Arms; generation, in your sleep you have been captured and mesmerized by My Enemy; surrounded by his lies you have been mesmerized and your memory, falling into oblivion, sunk into darkness, * but I, your God tell you:

sons! and daughters! you are

* Suddenly the Lord raised His Voice saying what follows.

5

the offspring of the Most High! you descend from Sovereignty and Splendour, oh come! you belong to Us!* you belong to Heaven .... you are of Royal descent, so why, <u>why do you listen to the Beast</u>? you are blessed in Our Image, <u>not</u> of the Beast's! you are all meant to walk in the courts of the house of the Mighty One, so, allow Me to clothe you in My Splendour; open your heart and I shall save you!

* The Most Holy Trinity.

6

allow Me to enter My dwelling place* so
that I may embellish it and when I
do, I will hurl you out as one hurls
out a net, into this desert and into
the valley of death to cry out in My
Name: "Love is on the Path of
Return; the Day of the Lord is near,
nearer than you think! repent! repent
and be glad, the trumpet of the sixth
angel will soon be heard to fulfill the
warnings of God; hurry and repent to

* Our heart.

7

obtain the Lamb's Seal on your forehead;"
this is what you will say; you will
be My Throne and I, the theme of your
praises and under the eyes of My Enemy
I will give you a valiant heart to
conquer him and his followers in this
battle of the end of Times; this is
all for now, daughter; I bless you and
everyone who is with you; My Name is:

the Amen ♡

Patmos. 23. 7.94

Vassula - of - My - Sacred Heart, I bless you;

8

treat Me as your friend; never abandon your mission that includes writing; give Me time to write, give Me time to pour on My altar* My blessings, My myrrh and My anointing oil, give Me time to cover you with My fragrance: incense; to appease the wrath of My Father pronounce His Name with honour and praise in the Assemblies; I will call*² and you should be aware of My call; have My

---

* We can be the altar to God.
* Call for a message.

9

Peace now and have Me in your mind *¹
and keep Me in your heart !...*² friends ?
hear Me; always remember this : the
Messiah had been persecuted, treated too as
an imposter, His disciples too; child ! you
are from Me and since you come from the
Messiah, you shall suffer too as He
suffered, not that I had not warned
you before, this is just a reminder ;

A ☧ Ω

* Which means the prayer without ceasing.
*² There Jesus stopped, then looking at me He
asked : " friends ? " He meant : " we are still on"
                                            a deal?"

10

29. 7. 94

My Lord, sing Your new song* to the nations,
sing Your new hymn* to every race.
Your song heals, Your hymn works great
miracles.

peace be with you, My child; I will continue
to compose and as the rain produces
fresh grass on the hillsides, so will I
produce spiritual food for the hungry and
the poor; and you, be My harp,
so that all the congregation of the faithful join Me in My song; so, rejoice
your Maker! blessed child, how your

* song and hymn are: True Life in God.

11

weakness amuses Me .... take My Hand and walk with Me, I will help you advance and accomplish your mission by giving you an energetic way* and greater encourage-ment; I will give you these graces so that you teach what I have given you fearlessly; and through you, will spread in every nation the fragrance of the Knowledge of Myself! I am the Beginning and the End and everything is

* Since then, I obtained special graces from our Lord and during my meetings I felt His Power-ful Hand. Even fr. O'Carroll noticed it, it was so obvious.

12

measured by Me ♡ ΙΧΘΥΣ 🐟

- Rhodes -   7. 8. 94

Lord, the tepidness*[1] is unbearable here.
— Have You noticed the result of my
folly?*[2]... see the threats I receive by
the public radio*[3]? see how they hatched
all these lies? Would I be living in the
middle-ages, I would have been stoned to
death, or burnt to the stake!

before you I stand all the time; in the
end, I shall triumph, so do not fear ....
I have fostered you, I have raised you

*[1] spiritual tepidness.
*[2] To love God to madness and announce it by
witnessing on the local T.V.
*[3] From 2 orthodox priests, who spoke against me.

13

to glorify My Name; the man of peace will understand My Message of Peace; I have in My Messages, passages which are well concealed and hard to understand, but these are for those of whom the prophet Isaiah spoke: you will listen and listen again, but not understand, see and see again, but not perceive ....'

these people are uninhabited *[1]; they also distort the Scriptures; remind everyone *[2] that they cannot serve two masters;

*[1] Meaning, their soul is like a desert.
*[2] The Rhodian & Athenian prayer groups.

14

the master of the world and Me, I, who
am the Master of the Heavens; remind
them that they should put in practice
what they have been taught by Me; do
not prefer your own pleasure to God. I
am Holy and I want you to live holy;
you must keep steady all the time
and not at times ..... the devil is
prowling around you and has <u>sworn to</u>
<u>deceive you all!</u> pray for your priests *
who are ever so weak; they look with-

* Those especially on the island of Rhodes.

15

out seeing and listen without hearing, in this state they are depraved in mind, therefore, deprived of this Message; do not then be surprised that they mistrust the lot of you and argue on My Words; they are as dear to Me as you are and I love them as much as I love all of you; respect them and pray for them; I will conclude by telling you: keep My Holy Rules and abstain from the things the world is offering you; do not give the Enemy a chance; do not feed yourselves

16

on things that are not holy, this is My
second warning; the first was spoken
through the mouth of she who writes down
My Love Hymn .... be upright and self-
controlled so that you remain in My favour.
these are My conditions of following Me;
do not oblige Me to tell you one day:
" you were not upright"; now, you are
well aware of My conditions, if you are
subject to Me, follow Me; do not ever
wreck the work I have done on others*

* Tempt the newly converted back into sin.

17

repent! and seek truthfulness; I tell you
truly: those who behave like pagans will
have their share because they do not
only behave like pagans but even applaud
others who join them; if I, who love
you, do not reprimand you, who will?
if I have given you all these instructions
it is so that I refresh your memories
and remind you that I Am is Holy;

ic ♡ Is. "Of the men of my people not one was with me".
63:3   Since the prayer groups of Greece have
not a spiritual director (priest) because no
one wants to shepherd them, Jesus Christ Himself
comes to shepherd them. All the priests turned against
the 2 prayer groups, calling them heretic.

18

8. 8. 94

Look, my God, I have been picked up by
Your good pleasure to become Your living
tablet, Your echo and Your harp. Since
I know, my Eli, that Your thoughts are
above my thoughts and Your ways are
above my ways, as the heavens are high
above earth, come and examine me
thoroughly. Come and check my heart, test
me with Your Fire and use Your arrows
freely on me. Make sure that I am not
on my way to disaster. Guide my
step on the road that leads to Your
Eternal Domain, for I long to walk
in Your Celestial Courts one day!

how I love your spirit .... My pleasure is
to continue to use you as My tablet, My
echo and My harp, however faint your
sound may be, I will do the rest; I

19

promise you that I shall display My glory to all nations through you; stand aside and allow Me to step in; I tell you, many will recognize Me in these Messages as the Most High; .... and I shall bring even pagans to desire Me;* My Spirit, like a soft breeze will touch them; I shall go to countries that never held My Name Holy; I will speak to people who never called Me or invoked My Name;

* That means: to follow the greatest Commandment of God.

20

Lord, open my lips and my mouth will only repeat the words You have given me.

yes! I will let the whole world hear Me; be submissive and I shall accomplish My Will in you; in the meantime I will continue to give you in secret* the teachings of My Wisdom leaving the philosophers' mind in awe, I will give back the proud what they deserve .... yes, I will confound the sages and put them all into such

* God means that when He comes to give me a message there is no one around me, no crowds. All is done in silence.

21

confusion that they would not know their left hand from their right one; today these very ones delight in their falsehood and in their tower of Babel; these scholars have bought this world and own everything * ....

Lord! do I dare remind You that they too are Your children?

I have not yet heard from them:

"there is no other god except You, Father!"

(This answer made my soul ever so sad ...)

* Hearing the disappointed and somewhat bitter tone of God, I felt He might flare up and I dared interrupt Him.

22

Lord, Scriptures say: " I am Yahweh and there is no other, I form the light and I create the darkness, I make well-being, and I create disaster, I, Yahweh do all these things ." (Is. 45:6-7)

Lord, You are Master of the heavens and of everything! You are the Holy One and surely You can shine on darkness to bring light and You are known of Your Infinite Mercy, why, I myself have experienced Your immense Tenderness. Surely You can make well-being from disaster?

.... My purpose will come about, I shall do whatever I please *....

What more could I tell You or do to convince You my Beloved?

* Is. 46: 10

23

though you are tired of so much travelling, I shall grant you one part of your request, if you continue to travel for Me, proclaiming all the Knowledge I have passed on to you;

I will travel for You Lord. I am unworthy, but how can I say it? How can I obtain from You the other part too?

.... you are too frail for this ....

Not if You are in me and present. Not if Saint Michael is at my side and our Blessed Mother covers my head with Her mantle!

24

you truly rely on Me then ...."*

remnant of My Son; your clothing
will roll in your blood .... this will bring
salvation and conversion to many; I
will, not before long, pour out My Spirit
as never before on them and from their
lying tongue I will put an upright tongue
which will acclaim :

"I belong to the Most High and Father
of all ; "

* I noticed a note of amazement from Yahweh
my Lord.

25

another one * will call himself by My
Son's Name: 'Christian', and on 'his'
forehead will be written My Son's New
Name ; — oh, Vassula, put in the
sickle and reap! hurry, and be attracted
by the splendour of My Work and
reap! reap vigorously with Me and never
be carried off by the world; My Voice is
sweet, My Image perfect; come, come in
your Father's Arms ; dust and ashes

* Way of speaking. Does not necessarily mean,
  just one.

26

but Mine, with a soul and a heart;
come Paraskevi,* I will preserve your sight ♡

A ☧ Ω

10. 8. 94

My Peace I give to you; I am the Lord
and willingly, I am providing you with
food from heaven; write My dove,

*   Paraskevi is my second name. Paraskevi in
Greek means Friday. This name, which is a common
name in Greece, was added by my mother in
honour of Saint Paraskevi, who is the saint for
healing eyes. When I was born, my eyelids
were stuck together. My mother was not sure if
I had any eyes. She prayed to St. Paraskevi making a
vow to call me with her name. After 3 days my eyes
opened.

27

write these words from Scriptures ♡

" if you remain in Me ♡

and My Words remain in you,

you may ask for whatever you

please and you will get it ! " (Jn. 15:7)

listen and write : in mercy I have pitied

you and this is why I am here to in-

struct the uninstructed and to give My

Law to the lawless ; I shall continue

to feed this generation on the heritage

of My Father in Heaven ; the Bread

that cures you comes from above ; the

28

Bread of instruction descends from heaven,
from My Father's stores; no one should say:
"I have nothing to eat;" here I am
offering it to you so that you do not
get tempted to eat what is idle and
deadly, that which comes from the
root of the world; My Spirit is
offering you life and peace; I am writing
these few words to you through My flower;

Lord, some of the Greek orthodox clergy do
not believe it is You who speaks because You
use the word "flower" to call me.

29

I know, but have they not read:

" .... the flower of their offspring had

perished ...." (Wis. 18: 12)

for these I say: ' open your heart and

you will receive light and you will

believe ;' now they are like a pitiful

lot wandering in shadows and gloom ;

in My Mercy I overlook many of their mis-

deeds, to give them time to repent !

come, My friend, I have not forgotten

what you have offered Me that day ;

the days are coming closer to this instant

30

when I can make good use of your offer;* until then I shall prepare you; My appearances will continue on you so that I encourage you; ah My child, what will I not do for you? — in the Tenderness of His Love, My Father covered your path with sapphires; a King, yet so motherly, a Judge, yet so tender and loving, the Alpha and the Omega, yet so meek; come, I and you, we? us?

Yes!

* Read message of 8.8.94

31

speak in My Name, this pleases Me and honours Me;

Lord, I love You and I enjoy every minute of Your Presence.

Me too I take delight in speaking to you in this manner;

This is constant my Lord, anytime and any-where I will be; it is always there with me this gift, isn't it?

yes! this is what the Father and I offered you; ah Vassula, one day you will appear in the Courts of My Father to-gether with Me; I shall not pluck My

32

flower yet though, not until My Plan on
you has been consumed; until then,
continue to drink My Blood and eat
My Body; the Holy One is with you ♡

ΙΧΘΥΣ ⵜ⟩

(Our Blessed Mother:)   18. 8. 94.

daughter, My Heart rejoices whenever you
join in the saints' prayers .... My dear
child, you are fighting * in the same
fight as all the saints in heaven; I
am present too, so let your obedience

*Spiritual fight, by prayer, love, obedience to Go

33

to God have no limits; look, accept all that God gives you; it is by His Hand for His Own generous purpose that He gives you the possibility, the freedom and the power to act for the revival of the Church; if you remain as an untarnished mirror, you will reflect God's Image and His Works will continue to flash on you so that every nation will read the Word of Life welcoming Christ with an open heart; there is so much healing left to be done, but be confident in the Lord for

34

He Himself is your Holy Companion; since you have been raised up to be with Christ, My Son, you must live a true life in God; let every thought of yours be on heavenly things; teach others to think of God, to speak of God and to desire* God, then they will realize that God is life, Joy, and Heavenly Peace; look, the days are coming when this special grace the Lord was offering the world will come to

*That is: to follow and live the greatest Commandment of God.

35

its end; Vassula, learn and tell these words from Scriptures to those who say: " we are not obliged by any canon law to listen to any prophecy * ...." tell them : Scriptures never lie, they say : " make sure that you never refuse to listen when He speaks; if the people who on earth refused to listen to a warning could not escape their punishment, how shall we possibly escape if we turn away from a voice that warns us from

* Our Blessed Mother means, the prophecies given in our times.

36

Heaven? that time His Voice made the earth shake, but now He has given us this promise: I am going to shake the earth once more and not only the earth but heaven as well;*" the retribution from heaven reserved for this godless gene-ration is at hand; I shall continue to stand by you all and encourage you to pray, fast and live a true life in God; I will continue, if you allow Me, to bring you closer to God ♡   I,' i Panayia *²

* H6 12:25-26   *² ♡ Blessed Mother in Greek.
Literal translation is; The Most Saintly.

37

bless each one of you ♡ and tell you,
My mantle I have placed on you to
cover you My little ones from the evil one,
who, like a lion, prowls around you
continuously ♡

19. 8. 94

My heart is ready, Lord, to serve and be
under Your Command. In the Courts of
the house of Your Majesty You allowed me
to assist on Your instruction. — Although
our knees are weak for Lack of food* You,
my God, in Your Infinite Mercy took pity
on us; You came to our help: " I have
reserved for You, generation, riches and
wealth; in time of famine I come." this Is

* Spiritually under - nourished.

38

what You have been trying to tell us all this
time. I give thanks to You, with all
my heart I give You thanks.

My Peace I give to you; in My Heart lie
many treasures and I have shown now those
inexhaustible riches to you; I love you,
never doubt of My Love; I had once said
that this Treasure would be reserved for
your times, these times when humanity is
at its lowest and when in its so
deplorable state, the Beast would be
permitted to tempt all of you; this is
why I am asking you to pray more, to

39

fast and to follow My rules; open your
heart to Me and die to yourselves; and
you, daughter, remain in Me; accept your
accusers and I will lift your soul to Me;
never judge, never weep over material
things that do not last, be good and
holy; I will teach you to be perfect if
you allow Me, My Vassula; continue to
announce and proclaim the riches of My
Heart to those to whom I send you
and do not be afraid of your accusers,
leave those to Me, My child; see how much

40

more you have to improve? by the way you live you will be able to attract others too to know Me ♡ (Then He spoke to the prayer group of Rhodes).

I want each one of them to remember always that I have raised them by grace; none of them merited any of My Graces, this is why I want them to read from Scriptures the parable of the publican and the Pharisee, so that their zeal does not turn to bigotry; learn that no one is good but God; no one of you is perfect

41

yet; you have still very much to learn :
you have to learn the patience of the
Father, the love and the meekness I
show to you all, the absolute holiness
and tenderness of My Holy Spirit; this is
all for now, daughter; bless Me and love
Me; I, Jesus, bless you, pupil of Mine ♡

ΙΧΘΥΣ 🐟

23 . 8 . 94

My Lord ?

I Am; little one, have My Peace; I have
come to you to find some consolation in

42

your heart; I have in My Heart a wound which is unbearable .... today the followers of the Beast are profaning Me in the Sacrement of My Love; Love is betrayed, spat upon and walked over; I am now in their wicked hands; do you know what that means? My Perpetual Sacrifice is in their hands; they are stoning Me and between them swore to abolish Me from within My Tabernacle.

look! the day is near when they will officially declare that I should be abolished from

43

within My Tabernacle and erect in My place an empty cymbal; .... and Daniel's prophecy will be fulfilled; daughter, never weaken in your faith and your fidelity, never sleep, never doubt; rest Me, My beloved, rest Me ic

Generation! You cannot say, no, never can you say to your Redeemer: " I am lying all alone on my own soil, with no one to lift me up, " when His Day comes. When with Fire, generation, you will be struck, burning and scorching, and your gardens will wither as well as your vineyards, do not say to your Redeemer: " bring me something to eat and to drink;" for it is now you will have to repent and stop fanning what is evil. And as for

44

the godless who profane our Lord's Perpetual Sacrifice and have Death as their friend, the Fire will rage fiercer than ever on you, unless the Lord hears from you your cry of repentance.

3.10.94

Vassula-of-My-Passion, live for Me; this should really be the purpose of your life now; I shall make your enemies, who are also My enemies, ashes on the ground; O soil! * yet with a soul, why do you grieve Me so much? could it be that you

* Jesus called out with agony to the world.

45

do not want your heritage anymore? ah....
Vassula, how I grieve on this generation;
I stretch My Hand to them in their
wilderness, to their withered soul I come
to revive it, but they never seem to see
My saving Hand .... come, delicate girl,
and prophesy in My Name and tell My
people of My new covenant, that the
days are coming now when Our Two
Hearts will be pierced again; My enemies
are going to storm My Sanctuary, My
Altar and My Tabernacle to erect their

46

disastrous abomination; there is going to be
a time of great distress, unparalleled since
nations came to existence; by force and by
treachery they will invade My House; Rebellion is already at its work, but in
secret, and the one who is holding it back
has first to be removed, before the Rebel
profanes openly My Sanctuary; O how
many of you will fall by his flatteries!
but My own will not give ground,
instead, they will offer their lives for
My cause; I tell you, with tears in

47

My Eyes : " you will, My people, be tested by fire by this 'invader ....." his siege-works are already spreading out in the world*; the lion has left his lair .... listen this time and understand : the invader is a <u>scholar</u>, these scholars who follow the Beast and who deny My Divinity, My Resurrection and My Traditions, these are of which Scriptures say: " being swollen

---

* Constant propaganda in various newspapers saying that the Pope is very sick, burying him alive before his time. This is a mal-icious way and brain-wash to prepare the way for the enemy to step in.

48

with pride, you have said : I am a god; I am sitting on the Throne of God, surrounded by the seas ; though you are a man and not a god, you consider yourself the equal of God .... " (Ez : 28, 1-2)

today, My daughter, I found an undivided heart; a heart where I can write these secrets that have been sealed, since they will cer- tainly be fulfilled now; so allow My Hand to engrave these words on your heart, daughter :

when he who crushes the power of

49

the holy people will place himself together
with these traders of My Traditions in My
Throne, his presence will be erected as a
God in the center of My Sanctuary; I
had warned you, I am still warning you,
but many of you listen without understanding .... today you are building, but I tell
you, you will be unable to complete your
work .... open your eyes all of you and
look at the conspiracy in My House ....
conspiracy and traitors go together: someone
who shares My table is rebelling against Me

50

and all the powers of My Kingdom; I am
telling you this now so that when the time
comes you will fully understand My words
and will believe that all along, I, God,
was the Author of these cries; I will tell
you now something that had been kept
secret from you, I will reveal new things
to you, things hidden and unknown to
you: many of you will lose faith and
will honour this trader, because he will
use flattery, and he, together with the
people of an alien god, the scholars of

51

your days, the ones who reject My Divinity,
My Resurrection and My Traditions will
trample on My Sacrifice; as men's heart is
weak, many will accept him for he will
confer them with great honours once their
heart acknowledges him; My Church will
have to undergo all the sufferings and the
betrayals I Myself had undergone, but
Scriptures once more have to be accomplished
when they say: "I shall strike the shepherd,
and the sheep will be scattered"*; however,

* Zc 13:7

52

obey this shepherd no matter what
happens, remain faithful to him and to
no one else; your shepherd will be struck...
and the wails of My people will pierce
the heavens; when nothing but rubble will
become of My city, the earth will be riven
and rent and will sway; while all this
is happening before your eyes, a spark
will burst out from the East; a loyal
hand will stretch out from the East
to defend My Name, My Honour and
My Sacrifice; while blasphemies will be

53

pouring out from the Beast's mouth, a heart will be offered from the East to save this Brother who will be the prey of the Evil one; and while treaties will be breaking, prophets repelled and killed, a noble voice from the East will be heard: " O Irresistible One, render us worthy of Your Name; may You grant us to be one in Your Name...." — Satan is on his way to My Throne; summon your communities and tell them that I, Jesus,

54

will dress your wounds when the time comes;
our Two Hearts will be your only refuge in
the days of your distress; so dearly
loved by Me, listen and understand:
I want you to be courageous, do not
fear in the days of this great tribulation,
continue to defend My Word, My Tradition,
and do not accept frills and human doctrines
which My Enemy, with his pen, will add
and sign; his signature will be in
blood taken from infants used for
their murdering initiations, these

55

initiations for his promotion! * .... and while, My friends, you will all be waiting for the Dawn, while treaties will be breaking and when Rebellion will be reaching its bursting point, lift your eyes and watch the East, watch for the Dawn; watch for the Light that will rise from the East; watch

* "His signature will be in blood ": Since so many nations have legalized the law of abortion, it is easier for Satan to obtain power. Abortion is a hidden form of murder, thus giving Satan a cult, since it is human sacrifice. To give power and promote the enemy, Satan demanded this hidden form of human sacrifice.

TRUE LIFE IN GOD

56

for the completion of My Plan; while
the thirsty man with his throat
parched will be looking for water,
I, in all My Splendour and Sovereignty
will descend upon you like a River
with My New Name ♡

ΙΧΘΥΣ 🐟

5. 10. 94

My Vassula, follow My rules; My rules
are to: reveal My riches to all mankind
and to allow My Spirit to be your only
Guide; do not lose courage, My Love

57

will sustain you; listen and write:

My earnest wish is that the West and the East meet; I need those two pillars * of My Church to come together and consolidate My Church; My Church cannot stand firm with only one pillar; I have commissioned them to safeguard My Church; but scarcely had I returned to the Father than your division took place, and My Body was torn by the creatures' hand that My Father created; since then, I was

* The West and the East

58

shaken by terrible sights; today, any
delicacy from the part of My creatures
to restore My tottering House touches Me
profoundly; any step towards unity, all
heaven rejoices; any prayer offered for
the restoration of My Body, My Father's
wrath diminishes; any gathering in My
Name for unity, My blessings are poured
out on those sharing these meetings ♡
My Eyes watch over those who love ♡ Me
and who, in spite of their imperfections,
carry out My fervent desires ♡

59

come then together, and together lay the Table to honour Me; you know the taste of My Cup and My Bread; both of you have been tasting My Meal, the third tongue though does not yet fully know Me; but you, you have been keeping My Tradition, you have been unshakeable; *[1] have you not heard: 'brothers and allies are good in times of trouble, better than either, generosity, to the rescue;'[2] hasten

---

*[1] Unshakeable on the Tradition.

*[2] Ecc. 40:24

60

the day, for My Glory; from the East
I will hasten a generous heart who in
its loyalty will seal a covenant of peace with
the West ♡ My Sovereignty was split in
two and from thereon into splinters ....
how glorious you were in your earlier
days ! come and rebuild My House into One
by unifying the dates of Easter ....
        there are two Sisters that My Soul
rejoices in and loves, although surrounded
by a crowd of their brothers, who
would not listen to them, even though

61

their soul* has never been so close to death, they would not listen; I, Myself, therefore, will bring the two together to honour My Name and pronounce My Name around one altar, and immediately after, the brothers all together will complete the ceremony; I have been looking with displeasure on these proceedings in My House and I tell you: a traitor will bind My Law and My Tradition and subdue the pillar that honoured Me in the West;

* The brothers' soul.

62

a census will take place without consult-
ing Me; their hearts are set to remove
this pillar before I bring together the
pillar from the Church of the East
and consolidate My tottering House, they
are set to inherit what does not belong
to them; how can they forget that
I search every heart to know what it
devises? My Spirit is longing to
bring you together so that My people,
who today walk in darkness, will see My
light, and those lying in the valley of

63

death may resurrect ♡

6. 10. 94

Do I do any good? Am I devout to You my
Lord?   (I caressed His hair on His
portrait of the Shroud and kissed His hair
and wondered whether these things offended
Him). Do I offend You?

no; I like it ♡ *¹ Vassula....ah Vassula,
how long will it take you to understand
Me ? *² My Love is Infinite ! .... now
My child, everything you do for My Interests
is for My Glory ; do what you can

*¹ He saw my hesitation.
*² Jesus said this with great humour.

64

and I will do the rest; never fear;
I know how much you can give, so
anything that will lack, I will give
and fill up the rest; I and you,
we, us, remember? so be in peace;
love is with you ♡ ic;

Excerpts from Notebook 74

9 October 94, NB p.1 . . . *Have I Not Written With You More Than One Hundred Notebooks For All Of You, To Teach You My Sound Knowledge?*
- ✠ I shall continue to use you as My mouthpiece till the end
- ✠ My people give less and less importance to My Blessed Sacrament
- ✠ Do not keep back My calls...allow Me to irrigate this desert before My Day comes

13 October 94, NB p.5 . . . *I Will Reveal To Them My Holy Countenance*
- ✠ I will appear often in your place
- ✠ I have come for the sick, the poor

14 October 94, NB p.13 (St. Michael) . . . *The Perpetual Sacrifice Will Be Trampled*
- ✠ The devil today...is given great honors...worshipped as a father
- ✠ Satan, today, is tempting even the elect of God
- ✠ Trouble is coming to this generation that constructs its towers with innocent blood

18 October 94, NB p.20 . . . *Offer Me All Your Oppressors*
- ✠ I have provided you...with a flame that no one will be able to extinguish
- ✠ My Father rules everything but not your freedom
- ✠ Even if there were to be tens of thousands posted by My Enemy against you, do not fear...My Presence is your Shield

20 October 94, NB p.29 . . . *My Father And I Will Continue To Scandalize Your Philosophers And The Haughty*
- ✠ I still delight in giving you My noble Knowledge...if you knew how it pleases My Father to give you Wisdom
- ✠ Do not say: "Where is my Jesus?" My beloved, I am all the time with you

✠ I am the Author of *True Life In God* and I shall prove it by appearing in your place

24 October 94, NB p.33 . . . *My House In The West Is Being Plundered*

✠ Many of your nation object to My Call of Unity...you the child of My Mother! Why, why have you become so obstinate?

✠ I had asked them to assemble under Peter...I selected Peter to feed and guard My lambs

✠ You have kept My Tradition...yet you put aside My two greatest commandments

✠ Do not weep bitterly over the Apostasy...for tomorrow you will eat and drink together with My Shoot from the Eastern Bank

✠ The East and The West will be one Kingdom...<u>I shall settle for One date</u>...I shall make one stick out of the two

✠ They will no longer practice alone, but together I shall reign over them all

25 October 94, NB p.51 . . . *Only The Lowly Will Rejoice*
At The Sound Of My Messenger's Footsteps

✠ This people approaches Me drunk with spite...so in their case, this prophecy of Isaiah is once more being fulfilled: "to the seers they say, 'see no visions' to the prophets, 'do not prophesy the truth to us'"

✠ In your silence you will hear My Voice

✠ I shall not impose Myself on you...I shall take each one by the sleeve and ask them: "Are you the child of the Father?"

✠ I have the power to make you a light for the nations so that My Salvation Plan reaches the ends of the earth

✠ I will refresh your soul and turn it into the perfect reflection of Christ

✠ Although you will still be among men, your mind will be in Heaven

I

9. 10. 94

Lord, I trust You. You are my Advisor, what a gift! What a gift to be able to serve a King! Open my heart to give ear to Your Knowledge so that I make Your Teachings Known to everyone.

Vassula, peace be with you; have I not written with you more than a hundred note-books* for all of you, to teach you My sound knowledge? you are going to minister for Me in My House; I will not fail you; I will send you My Advocate and He will remind you all that I

* This is the 74th notebook without counting 74 other notebooks that are my private messages and around 5 more of my angel's messages.

2

have taught you*; I shall continue to use you as My mouthpiece till the end; glorify your Holy One; let your mouth be like a sword and pierce open the hearts of mankind .... followers I need in these times and I have so few; sacrileges are augmenting, daughter, and My people give less and less importance to My Blessed Sacrament; pray to the Father that He may pour His graces on this

* He was telling all this just before my meeting.

3

generation; although many have turned their backs to Me, My Voice can draw them back to Me, so continue to be My Echo .... My lambs need to hear the Shepherd's call to return to the fold ♡ — I give you My command:

do not keep back My calls, for My Interests go before your interests; allow Me to irrigate this desert before My Day comes; allow Me to sanctify My sons and daughters; I have opened heaven's reserves to pour out on you, My Celestial

4

Manna, abundantly; I swore to leave no
one poor nor hungry, for My Blessings
are riches, My Love satisfying and the
Breath of My Spirit medicinal; leave My
gates open by showing Me obedience
and fidelity and many who have
fallen will rise and will go with
My Spirit proclaiming My Mercy
    come and draw from My ♡ Heart;
in here* lie all My Riches. your
weakness is ineffable, but what joy! for

* Jesus said this by pointing to His Heart.

5

I am King in your weakness; My Spirit will guide now your step; learn how I work; — be blessed you who carry My Word; ic

13. 10. 94

Here I am Lord, as ready as I can be to serve You, with honour and love.

peace be with you, soul; My Vassula, I will always give you opportunities to announce My Messages no matter how much your ....*   or put it rather that

* The Lord hesitated here, then said what follows.

6

way, _our_, persecutors try to stop you, they will never reach their aim .... I am Master of the heavens and the earth ...; blessed one of My Soul allow Me now to use your hand again. I will continue to talk to the nations through your mouth and to encourage you I will reveal to them My Holy Countenance now and then; and on you too I will reveal to your society your glorious body; these gifts are offered by My Father who loves you for loving Me; I will show to your

7

society the brightness of your glorious body;*¹ that one of which is imperishable ♡ ..... to show you My way into My Kingdom allow Me to sanctify you*²; I will continue to cure your sick and My Name will be praised; hear Me: to extol My Name I will appear often in your place as a reminder of My marvels and of the reality of My Presence; I will reveal Myself on

*¹ Many people in different countries witnessed this. They saw my face very bright, like porcelain, like light coming from within, and as though a young girl. *² By purifications, & trials.

8

you to show everyone how I am in you
and you in Me, that they may believe
that through your words, I Am; the
love with which the Father loves Me is
in you, My child, this is why I am in
you; having won the favour of My Father
in Heaven, He has now granted you
this gift, this inexhaustible treasure
worth more than all the treasures of
the world put together; I am coming
to you again so that you hear the
word of God; I am God; glorify

9

My Name and announce to this world
that I conquered: My miracles; I want
My miracles to be known and spread;
heaven and earth should see My Glory;
doubt no longer but believe now....
_ I will open for you an important
door *; hear Me now and write in My
Name: I tell you, salvation will come
to the abandoned, and to those who

* He did not tell me which door. But Later
on I understood. A few days later Fr.
O'Carroll managed in spite of all the obstacles
to have a private meeting with the Patriarch
Bartholomew in Constantinople.

10

never sought Me; the poor and the wretched; the abandoned and the starve *

need water and there is none; their tongue is parched with thirst; this is why I will give them water with My own Hand; have you not noticed how I am gathering the wretched? the dying? I will call the sinners and all those whom your priests *²

execute daily with their hard words;

* Jesus is speaking in metaphors. He means the unconverted, the strayed sheep and the uninstructed in spirituality.
*² Read note on page 11.

||

I shall turn their sadness into joy and when they will ask : " what about us? can we inherit your kingdom too ? can we really be saved ? " I will answer them : " your plea was heard by Me, I will save you too by your very wretchedness will I save you; I have come for the sick, for the poor,

* Note: Some who just got converted by 'True Life in God' in Greece and for the first time in their life go wholeheartedly for confession, and are eager to return to Church, thirsty for God, are condemned with harsh words by the confessor, if he finds out about the messages and sometimes menace them with ex- communication.

12

have you not heard this before, My child?" it is not those who call Me: "Lord, Lord," and do not do My Will that I will hear; it is not those who speak daily about your foundations, but have none themselves, that I will hear; alas for you who are rich! you are having your honours now, but at the day of your burial you will be stripped from My Kingdom and your name from the Book of Life ...

and you, daughter, do not let

13

your soul flutter elsewhere than in My
Heart ♡ do not fear to proclaim
My Merciful Call, honour My Spirit!
I will augment in you so long as
you are prepared to diminish, effacing
yourself; My Works on you will glorify
My Name, we, us? *ic* ;

14. 10. 94

(St. Michael speaks)

Vassula - of - Christ's - Passion, I, Saint
Michael the archangel, greet you and
bless you; — remember how God called

14

you to live a True Life in Him?
the memory only of your spiritual
resurrection, to this day, touches Me
to tears .... you were once at war with
God since all your concern was on what
is unspiritual, but now, glory be to
God, the Just, the Most High, He
has covered you with His Holy Spirit
and with His powerful Hand, lifted
you to become a witness of His Holy
Spirit, since His Spirit made His
home in you: and from the

15

beginning*¹, His Spirit finding His home in you, glorifies Himself by listening to your cry of: "Father, Abba";
— it will not be long now when He will descend to pull down iniquity that installed itself in men's hearts; look here, for over three years the Perpetual Sacrifice*² will be trampled; for this reason of incredible blasphemy, a third

*¹ The beginning of my conversion.

*² The real Presence of Jesus in the Holy Eucharist.

16

of your inhabitants shall die of iniquity;
the Lord swore this by His Holiness;
prepare yourself to meet God now....*

I have told you all this with no
pleasure, for the devil today, in your
generation, is given great honours;
he was a murderer from the beginning and a liar, and now he is
worshipped as a father; the honours

* When St Michael saw my sadness, He was
allowed by God to remain a little bit
more with me, for I was reflecting
sadly on the contents of His message.

17

are given to him instead; in your days, they bow low before his works and in this way, your generation has drawn down punishment on themselves; your countries are infested by legions of unclean spirits that roam everywhere; Satan, today, is tempting even the elect of God; this is why trouble is coming to this generation who constructs its towers with innocent blood* and founds its homelands on

* Abortion Law legalized in many nations.

18

crime; this sacrifice* alone pleases Satan....
put your trust in the Most High, child,
and encourage people to ask for My
intercession; Saint Michael, the archangel of God will never weary of

* The abortion pleases Satan, because
Satan needs human sacrifice to
gain power, and so abortion is practised daily with so many not even
being aware that it becomes a
free-giving cult to the Devil.

The Devil thirsts for blood and he
gets it now from the innocent.

19

defending the Truth ; stand your
ground , *   even though the Enemy's
blows on you can be traumatic ; I
am with you ; enjoy the favour of
the Most High ♡

* St. Michael was trying to tell me to 'copy'
Him, that means, I never to get weary
of writing or feel discouraged in
spite of the blows I receive .

20

The Lord speaks :

be in peace ; come close to Me and feel
My Peace ; I will never abandon you ; I
will help you so that My Heart triumphs
in you ; do not allow Satan to delude
you by doubting ; I will increase My Signs
on you to honour My Name I shall
do these things ♡ A☧Ω

18.10.94

My little child, I am Yahweh, your
Eternal Father ; far, far beyond this
maddening lot,* I have taken you,

* my oppressors

21

to be present in My Courts; be persistent
in your work and offer Me all your
oppressors; say:

> " Father, in your Righteousness,
>   deliver me from the lying tongue,
> come quickly, God, in Your great Love;
>   answer me, my Yahweh; "

and I am now saying to you:

My child, My child, even if there
were to be tens of thousands posted by
My Enemy against you, do not fear,
beside you I am to defend you; My

22

Presence is your Shield; who is like unto Me? to whom can you compare Me? with whom can you assess Me? My Presence is Splendour and Majesty; let no man oppress you; it is you, My child, who shall restore My sanctuaries* for Me; I have not appointed you for your fame, but for blessing My Name; I have not risen you for your glory but for Mine; I have given you a

* Sanctuaries here stands for: souls.

23

disciple's tongue to proclaim My Salvation Plan day after day .... set to
work, My seed, and I will be with you;
I have provided you already with a
flame that no one will be able to extinguish; I shall increase My prodigies
on you; I have, in My Own treasury
many more; I will give My prodigies
according to the measure you will receive
from your oppressors: My Son will appear
in your place, revealing Himself to your
society; can anyone say I am depriving

24

them of signs? can anyone say I am
not the Author of My saving and healing
acts? can anyone complain I am keeping
My right Hand hidden? who could be
but Me who gives a king's banquet
in this wilderness?* who could split
the rocks in the wilderness, quenching your

* "A king's banquet" stands for signs, prodigies from God, miracles and His Holy Spirit's
works, so lavishly poured on us.

25

thirst with unlimited water*, if it is not done by Me? open your eyes, generation, and concentrate on My marvels; and you, daughter, since I have set you free, guide My people into My House;

unite My people into My House, where they too, will obtain their freedom; unite My people into one heart; follow

* "Split the rocks" stands for God's power who can send His Holy Spirit like a River in the wilderness we have created.

26

this commandment :

let your lips bear witness to My Gracious-ness; enliven this dying flame*[1] and continue to build My altars*[2] and My House; no one will besiege My tent*[3]; there is an angry legion of demons who hide beneath other tents*[4] to go and

---

*[1] It means : this dying generation.

*[2] Altars stands for souls.

*[3] This means that no one will invade my soul, (tent) because it is the dwelling place of God and His property.

*[4] The word "tent" again stands for soul. God means that demons use people to perform their work.

27

uproot the hopes I have given you and fill you with terror, but disease will devour their flesh and worm will be their cover .... have My Peace and never cease praying for the unconverted;* My Heart pains Me, My child, for I see to the ends of the earth and what I see is not according to My Heart's desires ... your Father rules everything, but not

* Right there I felt God very sad and as someone who was weary. Then like a father who shares his pain and confides his sorrow to his child, God explained to me the reason of His sadness on what follows.

28

your freedom .... and man has perverted his freedom .... beloved, pray so that those who are dying will have time to redress themselves; every drop of love is used for their salvation; many who are beneath the rubble are still breathing,* so pray for them that I refresh their soul; remember, you are freed to free those from the rubble; come, I, Yahweh, love you, I bless you; A🔗Ω

* I also understood: barely breathing.

29

20. 10. 94

Lord ?

I Am; look Vassula, My purpose of raising
you is still the same: My Father and
I, visited you, educated you, yes!
I have raised you up; can you say
today that your knowledge came from
men ? or, from having studied theology?

Glory be to God, all I have learnt
    comes from You.

My Father and I will continue to scandalize your philosophers and the haughty
of your society through Our Works and

30

by the poor instruments We choose;
I delight in teaching you; yes, I
still delight in giving you My noble
Knowledge; ah Vassula,* if you knew
how it pleases My Father to give you
Wisdom .... so do not be unaware of all
these blessings; do not say: " where is my
Jesus?" My beloved, I am all the time
with you; My gaze constantly on you;
allow Me to progress you spiritually and
extensively, allow Me to flee now and

---

* Jesus sighed.

31

then from the wickedness of the world and
rest in your heart ♡   in your silence
I take My rest;   in your fidelity I am
King because what I receive is: honour and
praise; and in your love I am glorified;

Lord, you have schooled me giving me
strength; you have addressed me and Your
words lifted me. My food is You. Why
give this Gift of Light to someone so
wretched?

because I was struck by your wretchedness;
had I found someone weaker than yourself
I would have chosen him or her; your
wretchedness compels My Mercy to immerse

32

you; your wretchedness makes Me shake My Head .... weaker and more wretched than you I cannot find ... there is no one! how else would I have worked if I would have had to face rival after rival inside you? I find none .... and would there be any arising, as they would be coming I would blow them away with My Breath; so allow Me to hold your right hand in Mine .... do you feel happy My Vassula?

Yes! Very!

I love you for having allowed Me to

33

prosper you and through you others ; never
fear, My beloved ; so all I say to you now
is : love Me , write and continue to glorify
Me by witnessing. I am the Author of
True Life in God and I shall prove it
by appearing in your place ; it is My
Father's gift to you and to others ;

24. 10. 94

Vassula - of - My - Sacred - Heart ;* would it
please were I to say : Vassula - of - the -

* I was thinking that by calling me in this way, the
Orthodox will continue to turn against me because
the terminology is Roman Catholic.

34

Pantocrator? you are dedicated under My Name; I am 'One'*¹ and the same, but men have parcelled Me out; he who sows division reaps a harvest of destruction; he who sows prejudice reaps a harvest of folly; have you not heard, that the fool folds his arms and eats his own flesh away? all the flesh that was covering them is gone and their breath too, nothing remains out of them but dry bones; My Names are Holy*², but

---

*¹ He is the same Christ
*² Christ's different Names e.g. Pantocrator, Divine Heart, Ichthus, Alpha & Omega, Immanuel etc.

35

men have patronized Me and have expelled Me from My Own House, My Own city and now from My Own Sanctuary* : they are oppressing Me and weighing heavily on Me, overweening with pride they are content to live in a desert; but I mean, in these coming days to display the holiness of My great Name, which is, because of your division, profaned; I tell you, daughter, do

* Not only Christ is "thrown out" from His Own House because of a question of terminology, but in the West some have started to abolish the Perpetual Sacrifice.

36

you see how your people are living undisturbed, and in an appalling lethargy when it comes to work for unity?*¹ I will allow no more of this; I am going to reach out My Hand even to the remotest parts of your nation and overthrow these traders*² that hinder My people to unite; I have raised you to be a sign of unity, a sign of My Mercy, a

*¹ The Greek Orthodox 'skipped' many of the ecumenical meetings.

*² "Traders" signify in this context, those who look after their interests and not Christ's.

37

sign of My Power, but the passions of
their ostentatious pride has turned them
blind; today I can say: " let their bones
burn " and take revenge; I can widow
your nation, but in My Mercy and for the
sake of My Love I will raise from the
East at least one, who will say to his
brother *   "   come and tread on my
ground; come and eat from my table,
come and drink with me; my vats are
overflowing with new wine; let us pasture

* The Western Brother.

38

our lambs together and make an Eden of
our pastures; our God! see what our
hands have made out of Your Sanctuary!"
My House in the West is being plundered;
I had asked them to assemble under Peter,*[1]
but they have not understood and are doing
the contrary; many from within that House
are saying: "why is it that we have to
have a guide,*[2] especially this guide?" I
had warned you that cardinals will turn

*[1] Message of 3. 6. 88

*[2] Reference from message of 16. 5. 88

39

against cardinals, bishops against bishops
and priests against priests; I selected
Peter to feed and guard My lambs but the
spirit of rebellion, thriving now, has reached
its peak of rebellion; this was the great
Tribulation I was warning you of; * My
House in the West is being plundered,
but, the wind from the East will rise
and together with My Breath will strip
the plunderer; many members of your

* Reference from message of:
        16. 5. 88

40

nation object to My Call of Unity and
have accustomed their steps to walk their
own way; they call themselves rich, but then,
where are their riches? .... " how is it you
have become a degenerate vine? can you
say that you have not sinned? is there a
single place where you have not sinned?
you, the friend of My Saints! the child
of My Mother! why, why have you
become so obstinate? what are your endless ceremonies to Me when you give Me
praise by lip-service? yes, you have kept

41

My Tradition and this is why the sword
will not come to you, yet you put aside
My two greatest Commandments and do not
follow them; why do you separate Tradition
from Commandment?* should you cover
yourself with myrrh and incense I should
still detect the stain of your guilt; open
your mouth now and let Me feed you
so that you devour life; do not say:
" we will go our own way," return to
Me and acknowledge your guilt!" and you,

* It means: "Pay attention to those 2 Commandments as
much as you pay attention to the Tradition.

42

daughter, shout My Message aloud and
prophesy, say : "I know all about My
House in the West bank, near the
River of Life and I know too who in this
House remained loyal to Me; daughter,
what do you see outside this House?

I see a lion prowling outside that House,
and eager to enter Your House from
a side window.

yes; the lion left its lair; daughter,
a destructive spirit is roaming; angel
follows close on angel, to warn you all
and tell you that My City in the

43

West bank will be stormed by the ravager and with great violence that is, to oppose and contradict My Law, My Tradition and My Divinity; the whole country shall become a horror; your holy ones, My messengers and My prophets will be hindered to go on with their work .... and over you will spread a heavy darkness while the Enemy, who is a scholar, will be banishing My Perpetual Sacrifice, thinking his acts go by unnoticed with his secret sins; My Hand will descend upon him suddenly,

44

destroying him altogether; that Night had been foretold in the Scriptures; but he, together with others, have put their oath in the Beast's mouth joyfully, honouring only the Beast for having given them its power. woe to the worshippers of the Beast! they will be moaning and bemoaning; now, daughter, what do you see on the other side of the bank, My House of the East?

I do not see any City, and the Land is sandy and flat as in a desert; but I also see a green shoot springing from this desert.

45

listen and write: glory will shine from
the Eastern bank; that is why I say to
the House of the West: turn your eyes towards the East; do not weep bitterly over
the Apostasy and the destruction of your
House; do not panic, for tomorrow you
will eat and drink together with My shoot
from the Eastern bank; My Spirit will
bring you together; have you not heard
that the East and West will be one
kingdom? have you not heard that

46

<u>I shall settle for one date</u>?* I am going
to reach out My Hand and carve on a
stick the words : West bank, House of
Peter and all those who are loyal to
him ;   then, on another stick I will
carve : East bank, House of Paul, together
with all those who are loyal to him ;
and when the members of the two Houses

---

* I understood that Christ was referring to all of
His messages of unity, calling us all to unify
the dates of Easter.   This alone seems
to "settle" Him and satisfy His thirst for unity.
Christ promised us that if we unify the dates
of Easter, He will do the rest.

47

will say: " Lord, tell us what you mean now," I will say to them: " I will take the stick on which I carved Paul's name together with all those who are loyal to him and put the stick of Peter and his loyal ones, as one; I shall make one stick out of the two and I shall hold them as one; I shall bind them together with My New Name; this will be the bridge between the West and the East; My Holy Name will bind the bridge, so that you will exchange your possessions

48

across this bridge ; they will no longer practise alone, but together and I shall reign over them all ; — what I have planned shall happen, and should men say to you, daughter, that these signs are not from Me, tell them: " do not fear, have you not heard that He is the Sanctuary and the stumbling stone as well ? the Rock that can bring down the two Houses but raise them up again as one single House ?" this is what you will tell them, daughter; I, God, am with you;

49

I shall inundate with My Spirit many more
hearts ; come, I love you; have My Peace

A ✕ Ω

(This is my vision)

50

This icon represents on the left side St Peter and on the right side St. Paul. They are holding together, like two pillars, the Church. Within it is the Meal: the H. Eucharist (in my vision, the River of Life) Above them is Christ the High Priest and the Head of the Church.

51

25. 10. 94

The nearer you go to God, the nearer He will come to you.

flower, I Jesus bless you; pray, converse with Me and love Me; be with Me in this way; it is My enthusiasm to do this work with you; let it be your enthusiasm too;

Your conversation is sweetness itself and you are altogether adorable*

allow Me, Shoot-of-the-Vine, to be graceful to you and offer you My Heart

* Sg 5: 16

52

so that you inherit My glory and wealth;
approach Me, you who desire Me, and
I shall feed you offering to you
My Heart in the hidden form of
the Eucharist to transfigure you into
a living tabernacle ♡ inherit Me ....
you will be good now and write
down My previous messages; I, Jesus,
love you, and bless you; ic

      Later on I approached our Eternal Father.
My Lord, my Creator, I love You.
love Me and also feel loved by Me;

53

stay near Me and let your heart retain everything that I have given you*; with Me you will learn; allow Me to proceed with My Plan giving Me more of your time;

Am I obstructing You in Your Plan?
(He lowered His Gaze on me, looking straight at me)

can one so small be a hindrance to the Almighty?

---

* Although my memory is very imperfect, and am by nature forgetful, it is not the same when God teaches me. He only has to show me once something and I can never forget it.

54

A microbe can be a nuisance to someone much bigger than the microbe.

Vassula, you have not understood the meaning of 'small', nor have you gras- ped the meaning of My Mind;* you delight Me .... come, do not be so obstinate; rejoice in Me and take courage; Yahweh?

I Am; I am your Father; grasp the meaning of My Words; have you not heard how I stunt the tall trees

* I felt that the Lord was amused.

55

and allow the small ones to grow?
come, you have still much to learn....
I bless you and the mission I entrusted
you with ♡ A ☧ Ω

Lord, because You have given me an inch
or two of Life and commanded me to
repeat what You have given me, from that
moment on my life is threatened; how
many have hatched calumnies on me?
For no reason they attack me, arraign-
ing me for doing what I've been commanded
to do; why these plots against me?

peace be with you; I shall not desert
you; fear not; have you understood the

56

meaning of the Psalm you have read*? [1]
I have guided your hand to reach and
read this part of Scriptures;

But why do these people attack without
studying my case, reading Your message
or even meeting me to talk things
over?

because this people approaches Me* drunk [2]
with spite, every vision, every word

* [1] Ps 38:11-22
* [2] When Saul was persecuting the Christians
and Jesus appeared to him, Jesus did not
ask him: 'why are you persecuting the
Christians?' He asked him: " Why are
You persecuting Me?" then:" I am
Jesus, and you are persecuting Me."
When I'm attacked it is God they attack since
this Work is not mine.

57

uttered by Me will continue to be sealed so that My prodigies appear to them as nonsense; have I not said that only the lowly will rejoice at the sound of My messengers' footsteps? this is the reason they do not hear or understand when I talk; they look at one another without understanding, for in them I have put a sluggish spirit .... so, in their case, this prophecy of Isaiah is once more being fulfilled:

" to the seers they say, 'see no visions;

58

to the prophets, 'do not prophesy the truth to us'; (Is. 30:10) and now to you I put these questions : are you still willing to be My Echo? are you still willing to continue carrying My New Song*[1] in your mouth ? and are you still willing to bear the Cross of Unity with My Son, Jesus Christ ?

YES Lord!

soul ! fall into My Arms ! *[2]

[1] * Ap. 14:3
[2] * The Father's Voice was joyful .

59

(Suddenly, Jesus' Voice was heard)

daughter! your generous heart will satisfy My thirst!

(Then, the Holy Spirit, also, touched, spoke:)

blessed one, I will complete in you My Work and I will continue to set springs to gush in ravines; I will supply each soul with everlasting water ♡

(Immediately after the Holy Trinity spoke, there was a quick exchange of embraces The Father hugged me, then the Son and then the Holy Spirit.   At this exchange of embrace my soul never felt in more & total collaboration than at this instant, with my heavenly Family. I felt I belonged to them and to no one else.)

60

(The Father now spoke again)

daughter, if you are willing to obey My Will, I shall wield My authority across these people through obedience* and end the Apostasy; to maintain the holiness of My Name I shall take each one by the sleeve and ask them: " are you the child of the Father?" and when our eyes will meet they will cry out to Me: "my Father! am I still worthy of You? I have sinned, I have become

* That is by our obedience.

61

a leper, a degenerate shoot of the Vine, because of my disloyalty to You I have died and decayed long ago!"

(The Son spoke:)

but I am the Resurrection; I alone am Wisdom, you are part of My Church too and I can use you; I can heal you and appoint you too as a witness; I have the power to make you a light for the nations so that My Salvation Plan reaches the ends of the earth;* to-

* Is. 49: 6

62

day I shall send you My Holy Spirit to breathe life in you and restore you ♡

(The Holy Spirit continued now.)

I shall not impose Myself on you, open your door* and I shall shed My light in you; I can make you grow and give you speech to glorify Our Mystery ♡ in your silence you will hear My ♡ Voice instructing you about the Way; from a pagan I can turn you

* That is the door of the heart.

63

into a believer then give you the Knowledge
of Wisdom ♡ and if you remain faithful
to Us, I shall invest in you the
Treasures of Our Glory and release you
from your misery, so that you too in
your turn will come to your neighbour's
help ♡ to you I will reveal My Beauty
and My Holiness and you will be lost
in admiration at My Presence; I am the
Tree of Life, whosoever has Me planted in
him, has eternal life; I can turn your soul
into an Eden, into a Paradise; with My

64

Divine Light I can transfigure your soul into a sun, brighter than all the constellations put together, for I am an inaccessible sun; you may have an incorruptible body if you allow Me to remain in you, and like a breeze in you I will refresh your soul and turn it into the perfect reflection of Christ; and although you will still be among men, your mind will be in heaven, and although your body will be moving among men, your soul and

Excerpts from Notebook 75

9 November 94, NB p.4 . . . Daughter, Pray That The Prophecies May Be Quickly Completed

✠ Alas for...those who walk with the outward appearance of religion but reject the inner power of the Church!

11 November 94, NB p.18 . . . While You Speak I Am Glorified

✠ How much more could I prove to you that this is all My Work?

25 November 94, NB p.20 . . . Message For France

✠ I shall never forget how you were My pride and...how obedient you had been—What has happened to the utter zeal you had then?

✠ I will respond to your cry of repentance

1 December 94, NB p.23 (Rome) . . . Today, Rome, Your Soul Has Turned Into The Beast's Reflection

✠ You have rejected, disowned and raged at My messengers...many of My sacerdotal souls...have sworn to crush them

✠ You claim to have knowledge and discernment...so as to tarnish My mouthpieces who expose your darkness to the world

✠ The outcome will be My Promise: the New Heavens and the New Earth

7 December 94, NB p.35 . . . My Crown Of Glory Will Be Offered To Me From The East

✠ I will reveal more and more My Son's Holy Face on yours

✠ Tell this generation how I abhor their wisdom...although they have become more like wild animals than saints...I still burn with love for them

7 December 94, NB p.44 . . . Unite The Dates Of Easter

NB 75

16 December 94, NB p.48 . . . My Teachings Are Meant For All Of You

✠ I have not been teaching you merely to instruct you alone...I will guide your hand and My Voice shall be heard by many

18 December 94, NB p.50 . . . I Need Sacrifice, Generosity And Love

✠ I am gaining so many souls!

Message For Argentina (NB p.55)

✠ Open your heart, not your mind

✠ So long as you have your eyes fixed on the world you will not see the grandeur of My generosity...being poured on you to save you

✠ The God whom you have forgotten has never forgotten you—today I invite you at My Table...come...you will benefit from the Riches that My Sacred Heart offers you

24 December 94, NB p.57 . . . I Want You To Be Faithful To Me

✠ Learn from Me to save souls for Me

✠ My Father and I will display Our Holiness in you to strengthen you

26 December 94, NB p.59 . . . So Many Souls Are Heading Into The Internal Fires

✠ Be vigilant and use the discernment I have given you

✠ I will augment your perseverance with this (sign of My Love) on you

27 December 94, NB p.62 . . . My Return Is Imminent

✠ ...even nearer than it was when you were converted

✠ I will continue to build My Plan in you until it is completed...the poor will hear something never told before and will see My Holy Countenance on you

✠ Those whose eyes were veiled will see all My Glory

✠ Whosoever will be moved by My Spirit...the Father will welcome him...with throngs of angels in Heaven

1

mind will be as an angel's, walking in the Courts of Our Kingdom, walking among angels; if you open the door of your heart to Me, I will set your heart aflame and free it from the defilement of your passions; I shall frequently set your heart aflame to burn all your passions no matter how small, that keep you prisoner to this earth ♡ I am the revelation of the Son and the Son is the revelation of the Father* and the

* "To have seen Me is to have seen the Father". Jn 14:9

2

image of the Father; anyone who has
the grace and sees the Son, sees the Father,[*]
and anyone who perceives My Holiness
perceives the Son and the Father, come and
inherit the Way; We will carry your
mind and soul and heart in Us to
live in Us and flourish you, breaking
all the boundaries that held you prisoner
to this world; come! come and inherit
Our Splendour; We will carry you, like

[*] "Do you not believe that I am in the Father
and the Father is in Me?   Jn. 14:10

3

the bridegroom who carries his bride
over the threshold into his nuptial chambers,
We will carry you too into Our Kingdom, and I
shall pour on you and sate you with
My ineffable blessings*; to maintain you
alive I shall teach your spirit to cry out
to the Father: "Abba!" I will teach you
to live in Us, move in Us and breathe
in Us; I shall teach you that We are
Life and in Us you will not cease to
be ♡

* gifts

4

Blessed is the one who passionately desires
You for he will possess You, and thus
will be thrice blessed.   Marvel of
my life, what have I done to possess
You?   Immortal Splendour, indes-
cribable to express with words, what
have I done so that You unite me to
You?

(Christ spoke.)

I wanted you to become My companion
in Love ♡ come;

AℵΩ

9. 11. 94

My Vassula, I give you My Peace; listen
and write: as you know, he who touches
you unjustly, touches the apple of My Eye;

5

stand firm though, My child, and pray
that faith be restored in your country,
for faith is not given to everyone ♡
I am the Author of My Message ♡ and
I will see that it spreads quickly; this
is My Work and all that has been un-
done by human hand will be restored
again by My Hand; as for your oppressors in your country do not regard them
as enemies but as people who are also
part of the family and therefore, dear
to Us*, needing prayers; let your love
* Holy Trinity

6

increase and not decrease, so that when
I come to call you, I may find in you
the same love I Myself have for you;
My desire is to find you fit for My
Kingdom; accept your Cross and let the
Father repay those who are injuring you;

(The Holy Trinity spoke :)

ever so dear to Us, imitate Us ♡

(The Holy Spirit then only spoke.)

I will continue to direct you and give
you My Instructions to be suitable for
Our Kingdom ♡; during My Instructions

7

to you I will teach you to lay hands on
your brothers and sisters so that their
spirit falls in My embrace; the dead* are
going to be raised; I shall lift them,
though not all; it is I who give you
life and breath; have you not heard
that it is in Me that you live and move
and exist? I will continue to train you
spiritually in My Love, in My Infinite
measure, so that your motives become
those of Our reflection and through your

* Spiritual death.

8

mouth I shall continue to speak and
raise many of your dead; it is the
Father who sends you out travelling; I
am with you though all the time;
soul! I shall continue to model you
according to Our Image so that when
your perishable nature must perish I may
lift you once again*, to walk into Our
Courts; trust Me, Vassula, and allow Me
to flutter freely in you; allow Me to

*¹ The ¹ˢᵗ resurrection was of the spirit, conversion.
This resurrection is of the dead.

9

breathe in you so that I can continue
to teach you with Wisdom and counsel;
everything I do, My infant, is not of the
letter but by My Infinite Holiness and
Glory; My Knowledge embodies the Truth;
come and possess the Truth and all
that I own, it is freely given to all mankind; seek My goodness, My patience
and My tolerance so that in your weakness these gifts may lead your mind
and your heart to a greater repentance;
yes, live holy as I am Holy .... be holy in

10

every one of your actions and do not let
Me flee from My dwelling place * for lack
of holiness; let your loyalty to Us
grow as Our loyalty, *² to preserve you from
falling into a lethargic spirit and back
into the evils of the world; let your
joy be in Us; daughter, pray that
the prophecies may be quickly completed
and that I, the utter fullness of God,
the utterance of your spirit, the light
in your eyes, descend in your midst

* The Spirit dwells in us. *² Between the Trinity.

||

to show the world how wrong it was,
to show to the churches their iniquity
of their division and how, although
they declare daily that there is one
Lord, one faith, one baptism and one
God who is Father of all, over all, through
all and within all, are uncharitable
with one another; We cannot say: " you
have done everything to preserve the unity
I offered you in the beginning when
you were still a child* and in My Arms;

* The primitive church.

12

today you say: " I am not a child any
longer" and I can walk by myself;"
and since then you stepped out of My
embrace and accustomed your steps to
walk your own way .... O child of the
Father! fruit of the Son! My City and
My Bride! * your fragrance left you ....
are there going to be any survivors left in
you when I will descend in full force?
I am standing at your doors, knocking,

* The Holy Spirit is talking to the Church.

13

if anyone of you hears Me calling and
opens the door, not only will I come
in to share his meal side by side, but I
will also engrave on their flesh My new
Name; they will call My Name then,
and I shall listen to them and I will
say once more: " these are My people, a
holy priesthood and I will live among
them all; " have you not heard?
" all flesh is grass and its beauty like
the wild flower's; the grass withers,
the flowers fade, but the word of

14

the Lord remains for ever; "* so why do
you call yourself " God" and enthrone
yourself in the Sanctuary? come and
repent and allow Me to guide you back
into your divinity; if you allow Me to
be your Torch and Light, no worldly
law can touch you. come and inherit
Our Kingdom in the right spirit; ask
for My gifts and I shall give them to
you: how can you say to your soul:

* Is. 40: 6-8

15

"soul, you have plenty of good things now, take things as they come: have a good time and roll in your wealth, obviously the inheritance is yours;" alas for your adultery! alas for your slanderous accusations that have been made by those who walk with the outward appearance of religion but reject the inner power of the Church! they are really members of the evil one, never realising that they are a wilderness and a drought, a walking wretch, pitiably

16

poor and naked too; how could you believe I could live in you* and offer you My gifts, you who are in debt to sin? have you not heard how I shun deceit? — ah Vassula, how so few know about Me and yet it is I, who hold all things together, am everywhere and know everything to the depths of God ♡ — let your love grow in Me and your joy be complete in Me so that your spirit sings praises to Me;

* The members of the Church

17

let your heart be in peace with Me and
your spirit forgiving; bear with patience
the Cross entrusted to you for all
you do does not go in vain; repay
wickedness with kindness; repay evil with
goodness and love; be mindful to the
poor and the wretched to give glory to
Me; be loyal and trustful only to
Me your God; alone you are not; I,
the Holy Spirit, am your life and the
one who directs you into Our Kingdom;
pray without ceasing and be holy in

18

My Presence ♡ A ☧ Ω

11. 11. 94

Lord?

I Am....

Lord, when liars hound me You must help me!
(Ps. 119 : 86)

name Me anyone who can stand up to Me;

There Is no one like You.

so then trust Me .... I shall chase your

oppressors away and I, Myself, will take

up your cause; I am with you so whom

do you need more?

19

Holy are You and Mighty; Your Presence
are Splendour and Majesty, I need no
one but my Maker.

I swore never to abandon you; Branch
of the Vine, how much more could I prove
to you that this is all My Work?
Soil! give your harvest now, speak!
pass on without reserve what you learned
from Me; while you speak I am glorified and you sanctified ♡ you are indeed
in My Hand; I will continue to help you
and keep your memory fresh; so now
let "us" rest; I in you and you in Me; ic

20

- France - 25. 11. 94

My Lord!

I Am; lean on Me.... peace My child;
listen and understand: depend on My massive
power and in My Infinite Mercy; preach the
the way I preached to you; follow the
heart of the Law*; I will remind you of
everything that has to be said;

(Then Christ gave this message for France.)

in these days I have taken sackcloth to
manifest My grief, have you not noticed
how I have taken the desert in search

* That is: Love. "Evangelize with love for Love."

21

of My eldest daughter*? today if I have
taken the desert in search of you it is so
that I test the genuineness of your name,
as you were the first chosen, to expand
My Love; I shall never forget how you
were My pride and My boast and of how
obedient you had been; — what has
happened to the utter zeal you had then?

* Title given to France.

22

I was once appealing to your heart ♡ how could you have forgotten all the graces you obtained from Me, only yesterday? you are heiress, Daughter-of-My-Church, to My Kingdom; I have come to you, to revive your devotion to My Sacred Heart, through a promise;*[1]

Gift-from-My-Father! once guardian of My Interests, do not compel Me to say: "My Property has been given[2] away and administrators have filled

* France has to promise to the S. Heart: Fidelity
* Sold away.

23

her, instead of allowing My Spirit to keep His seat, My seat is being ruled now by flesh; come back to Me and set your heart right again; repent and acknowledge your sin in the Presence of My Father and I will respond to your cry of repentance;

From p. 27. message for ROME —   1. 12. 94
Lord, my Refuge, my Comfort, my Smile
my Fountain, my Universe, I love You.

peace be with you; need Me, I am the Source of your life, I am the source of your

24

joy; need Me as you need the air which you breathe; do you wish to sit at work today with Me*?

yes! yes! My joy and my life is God Himself, the God who loves me. Come and help us in this Hour of Crisis, there is no such help from man!

daughter, raised and formed by Me, there are so few who listen, sin is still alive in their hearts, pride is governing them; your generation is heading for a blood-bath; I shall not remain hidden much

---

* Jesus means, under His dictation.

25

longer : My Justice will take over now ;
I have never ceased sending you My mouthpieces to warn you, yet to this day you
have rejected, disowned and raged at My
messengers ; many of My sacerdotal souls,
those who govern in high seats have sworn
to crush them ; I have taken all means to
reach this unfaithful generation to save it
and whisper in its heart some sound sense,
but My Spirit is persecuted by their spirit,
odious, those whose allegiance is wicked ;
I have again and again given them signs

26

of My Love but they have flung My Love
under their feet _ this is why I shall come
down to break the power of the wicked
and it will be <u>Me</u> who will persecute the
wicked till there are none to be found!
I turn away My Eyes from the world
not to look any more at their wickedness
and on those who say:" in our tongue
lies our strength; our lips have the ad-
vantage; who can master us?"* spite now
egoism and iniquity stand high

* Ps 12:5

27

among the sons and daughters of men ....
My Assemblies of My holy ones in heaven
mourn for the image they have taken ....
they have exchanged Our Image* We had
given them which identified them as sons
and daughters of the Most High for
the image of the Beast .... today the
more I call to them, through My mouth -
pieces, the further they go from Me;
²* you were once My Eden, Rome, My
Garden of delights, even My angels were

* The Most Holy Trinity's Image.
²* Rome's message.

28

lost in amazement over your perfect beauty
and you governed My House in holiness
and justice; honesty and love was the
soul of My House; you were indeed the
reflection of My Eternal Light, leaving an
everlasting memory to My saints and My
angels; your wealth and your treasures
were heavenly then; today, Rome, your
soul has turned into the Beast's reflection
and you have taken the position of
sentry in My territory to prohibit the
entry to My Holy Spirit and the prophets

29

who prophesy in My Name calling you for repentance and to renounce your evil ways; to save you, I, Myself, come to your door <u>now</u> to address you; have you not read: " a child of God listens to the words of God *;" but so far not a single word I pronounced has penetrated into you; for you, My Words are something inactive and nil; My grace has been rejected and My salvation plan discredited; you are outrageously rebellious and arrogant;

* Jn 8: 47

30

when it comes to the truth, this is
why you claim to have knowledge and
discernment on My heavenly Works so as
to tarnish My mouthpieces who expose
your darkness to the world...."

and you, daughter, never present your
defence; there are many witnesses who can
support you but the greatest one of them all
is My Holy Spirit ♡ put your hope in Me
who have the power to save you; if they
continue to ill-treat you unjustly, be
very humble, since the punishment ↟

31

reserved for them will be fire; you ought
to expect repulse and set-backs; for sin
has gained a hold over them .... continue
to declare the greatness of My Name to every
nation, I am sending you, so, 'lo tedhal!'*
yes, do not fear!"*2 I will continue to pour
out My Holy Spirit on you all and display the greatness of My Love; have you
not read: "when new wine is found in a
bunch of grapes people say: 'do not destroy it, it contains a blessing;" (Is. 65: 8)

* 'Lo tedhal,' in Aramaic means: 'Do not fear!'
*2 Continuation of Rome's message.

32

I shall do the same for the sake of
those who serve Me in righteousness and
are obedient to the one* who holds back
this Rebellion in My House; I refuse to
destroy the whole; but trouble for the
bloodstained hands! and you, you who
have taken the position of sentry to prohibit My Holy Spirit from entering in His
territory, I will send the most bar-
barous of the nations to surround you;
I shall drop in your desert a fire of

* The Pope.

33

fury, with a cloud that will cover your cities : thus your dark epoch will come to an end ....

My Lord, what is to be the outcome?

the outcome? the outcome will be

My Promise :

the New Heavens and the New Earth ....
Rome, who had ever shown such determination as Mine, to save you? My glory is rising on you, though night still covers you; above you My splendour appears, how is it that you cannot tell the times

34

nor the signs? I have not yet heard from
My House their cry of repentance; even now
they are not listening but lay traps for
My mouthpieces; were they to listen and
repent they would be able to turn many
from their evil ways and from the wickedness of their deeds that brought them
to apostatize! they never pause to consider
that I know about all their wickedness
and so not until they come to confess
their guilt and seek My Holy Spirit,
will I relent"... come, daughter, let

35

us go ♡   ΙΧΘΥΣ ⤳⊃

7. 12. 94

Yahweh how long will this exile last? But
I know that Yahweh is tender and as tenderly
as a father treats his child so Yahweh treats
me. Pull me out of the calumnies they have
spread about me for You are my Arbitrator.

lean on Me! I, Yahweh will console you ....
My seedling, I have formed you in My Courts
to become My Echo and My powerful mouthpiece; a sword for My Enemy*; do not be
afraid; was it not I, Yahweh your Abba,
who rescued you? do not be afraid, you
are Mine and I am known to protect My
* Satan and his like.

36

Own .... should your oppressors hold assemblies against you, I will be with you; or should they falsify My Message, calumniating you, for My Name's sake I will reveal more and more My Son's Holy Face on yours* to your society, as foretold; your oppressors will not drown you, I will always lift you to delight My Heart! should they assemble altogether as one great force to crush you, you will not be crushed, because you

* Phenomenon that happens whenever God wants. Even on Video-tapes it happens.

37

are precious in My Eyes; the Spirit of Wisdom
and insight was promised you to stir up your
heart and those of others; have you not
taken in account My triumphs? from
the depths of My being, I, Yahweh, love
you; let your oppressors come forward and
explain to Me your knowledge of My Knowledge .... listen, daughter, for your sake, I
will bring your brother from the East
to honour My Name; take courage now;

* True, many many conversions. Miracles. And in spite
of calumnies and strong persecutions, the Message is
well spread in the world and known. Translated in
29 Languages by volonteers.

38

a shoot of hope will spring from My
Eastern House; while the people will be
bullying each other, while human pride
will be growing to a bursting point and
while your lands will continue to be infested
by a spirit of rebellion, corroding like
gangrene in My Western House, remember,
what I, God, have told you long before
this happens :

My crown of glory will be offered
to Me from the East;
it is on account of this that I need

39

your cooperation, daughter, your immolation for My House; your hardships will be many, My child, but bear them with dignity to honour My Name and through these, in the end, I will triumph ♡

I will raise My offspring from the Eastern House to bring forward unity and in the end all the nations will assemble under One Name .... – in the beginning* My Son asked you, daughter, which of the two houses were more important, your house

* Back in 1986

40

or Our House; your answer honoured Me, and I turned then to My angels and told them: " for <u>this</u> answer coming from a corpse*, I will hasten her recovery and her cure will cure many .... I will confide in her the Interests of My House and she will be-come My theme of joy, My pleasure and My song, and I will send her out to proclaim in My Name My Messages of Peace and Love to all the nations of the earth, to the saints as well as to

* Spiritually dead.

41

the sinners : 'hear from Heaven, repent and forgive! if you return to God and praise His Name and pray without ceasing you will be forgiven !' this will be her theme ; " ah, yes ! My Vassula, I knew you before you were born and I knew I would be sending you in the middle of Plague *' ; this is why, I and you made a pact from the beginning to prepare you for your mission *3 ; this is why I had asked you that as soon as you were born, to fast *2 ...

*1 Ap. 6:7, – 11:6 – 13:12 – 16:2 – 16:11
* Ap. 15: 12   *2 By having my eyes shut for 3 days and 3 nights. My eyes were not opening. *3 continued on page 46.

*3 continued on page 46.

42

I made your soul swear an oath before My Altar, to remain in the dark for three days and three nights; now then, tell this generation, how I abhor their wisdom, and although they have become more like wild animals than saints who are to My likeness, I still burn with love for them; I am your God and you, generation, although so anxious to defile My Name, you are My offspring; the days are coming when one will say to the other: "how I envy these dead, how I wish I was one of them ....

43

why was I among those who were like a
brand snatched from the blaze?" today
I am speaking in the heart of My Sanctuary:
" the word that I announce is not for
your condemnation but to restore your
soul and save you;" and you,
daughter whom I have chosen, I will help
you, this is a promise from the Holy One;
I will put with you an angel who, when
you run you will not grow weary, when
you walk never tire, for he will carry
you on his wings, and I, for My part,

Page 310

TRUE LIFE IN GOD

Notebook 75

44

will renew your strength; courage, daughter
I bless you;

A ☧ Ω

7.12.94

Jesus Christ what can I do for You?

love Me .... let your heart be My fragrance,
fragrance that will draw My House into
one, fragrance that can bring My shoot
from the East to call out: "the Amen
wants His Promise to be fulfilled, the Risen
Christ is at our very doors with sorrow in
His Eyes .... for we have doubled His
agony, His Cross, and His Crucifixion; the

45

Holy One is at my doors, Brother,* like
the Appearance to His disciples, He tells
me:' peace be with you; as the Father
sent Me. I am sending you²*, go now and
meet your Brother and unite the dates of
Easter, then I shall give you the gift of
love and restore your sight; I do not
want you to perish in your own folly;
double indeed is My grief; double is My
groaning; go now and alleviate My pain,
brother, go and glorify Me by unifying

¹
* Roman Catholics   * Jn 20:21

46

the dates of Easter"; Vassula, in the end Our Two Hearts will triumph ♡ IXΘΥΣ ⤝◯

Later on, I was called by Yahweh to continue the message of the 7. 12. 94, and add this part on p. 41.

yes; write after,' to prepare you for your mission', for you are among those I am sending for this great war you had seen in the vision I had given you in the beginning; the battle of My Great Day* against the three foul spirits who ape

* Ap. 16: 14

47

My Holy Trinity, forming themselves into a triangle, △* these three foul spirits taking a corner each are alias the dragon, the first and the second beast; the great dragon, the primeval serpent, known as the devil or Satan, will continue only for a very short time now, to lead the world astray; and the power and the authority he is giving to the beast together with the second beast alias the false prophet, will be brought down and I shall triumph ♡ (Then one should read,

The sign of the Beast where we see this delta on buildings and in letters on buildings, as well as other places.

48

'this is why I had asked you' etc.)

16.12.94

I give you My peace; never let loose of My clothes, hang on to My hem .... My Spirit will give you strength, perseverance, courage and a flame to enflame other hearts; I tell you: no one who glorifies Me is let down by Me, no one who waters a parched land is ignored by Me; My Heart is too sensitive and pure not to be touched ♡ My graciousness observes you like a mother, like a father, every aspect of your

49

behaviour is observed by Me; I love you, have no doubt of My Love; you are My pupil and I, your Teacher; I have not been teaching you merely to instruct you alone, but My Teachings are meant for all of you....

Wisdom is your Holy Companion; ecclesia will revive; do not abandon writing; My Hand will guide your hand and My Voice shall be heard by many, for this is My Will and it will be done: and you, daughter, love Me, desire Me and write: be My Echo, do your best and I will

50

do the rest ♡ A⳨Ω

18 . 12 . 94

Lord! You have plunged me to the depths
of the Night, to its darkest, deepest
place You have plunged me. Why do
You hide Your Face from me? How
can I hear the marvel of Your Voice in
the dark. I stretch out my hands
groping for Your Hand, for the hem of
Your clothes, but I find nothing where I
can cling on.

My Love for you has no limits; if you
are going through the terrors of the Night
do not fear .... My Vassula, I am
with you — I am with you; I get My
comfort in your distress; you are My

51

comfort; My head-rest and My garden;
let your heart pine away with a longing
for Me; do not be envious of your en-
vironment and do not allow your heart
to talk nonsense; out of faith you
come to Me, what more prodigious from
all the prodigies? I tell you, you will
have your reward in the end; I have
appointed you as My Echo to repeat several times the words I utter; are
you genuinely doing your best to please
Me and serve Me?

52

If I am, it is thanks to Your Spirit of Grace.

look, today I have set you over so many nations, to be My Echo and revive My Church, to unite and embellish My Church; My reign on earth is near and to rescue My flock I need sacrifice, generosity and love .... see for yourself: how slight your efforts have been to win so many souls! I guarantee to you, that having your soul in the terrors of the Night, I am gaining so many souls, yes, thanks to your

53

acceptance I can enjoy My garden even more now; My bride, I am King in you.... child -of- My- upbringing and formed by My Divine Hands, I tell you: My Church will break into joyful cries one day, because in My everlasting love I will end this Apostasy quicker than foreseen;

Yet the worst has not come ... the worst has to come, nothing can be brought forth all at once; My Father will reveal His Mighty Hand to the

54

poor, but to the apostates and to the Rebel, a hurricane of fire from the east will scorch them because of all the filthy things they have done .... the culprit will die for his guilt; if he converts before My Day and restores what he has been destroying and acknowledges his sin, I will forgive him and he will live and not die: this is My Law thrice Holy;

SS

Argentina   18. 12. 94

write: Argentina! Argentina, you are Mine!
open your heart, not your mind; lift
up your eyes in heaven and you will <u>see</u>
My glory, My splendour and My sovereignty, but so long as you have your
eyes fixed on the world you will not
see the grandeur of My generosity that is
being poured on you to save you ...
I shall not weary of courting you, for
I have taken in consideration your charitable act * which was taken as far as
* The generosity and faithfulness Argentina
showed for the apparitions of San Nicolas.

56

you could; I am coming to tell you
that the God whom you have forgotten has never forgotten you; although
you only knew Me from the outside,
you are blessed; – today I invite you
at My table; come and let us meet
heart to Heart and you will benefit
from the Riches that My Sacred Heart
offers you; without these*, you cannot
live ♡

* Jesus was talking about the mystery of
the Eucharist.

57

24. 12. 94

Lord, Teacher and Saviour?

I Am; I have preached to you heart to Heart, to conquer you have I done these things, I wanted My pupil to learn from Me to conquer souls for Me ♡ I love you all eternally .... ♡ pupil, I want you to be faithful to Me; this is the gift you can offer Me during midnight Mass! — your fidelity; from your heart; and if you do, My Father and I will display Our Holiness in you to strengthen you in this battle of

58

the Plague*; shall any of the followers
of the Beast be hostile to you, be
like a sling to them and shatter them
as in the vision* I had given you ....

* Ap: 15: 12 - 6:7 - 11:6 - 16:2 - 13:12 - 16:11

*2 The vision: I found myself held by the
followers of the Beast. They took off my
crucifix - ring, disappeared for a while
with it and then came back with it. They
gave it back to me. When I took it I knew
that they had profaned it. — Then they
accompanied me to their door to leave, but
as I was passing by in their hall they had
the Emblem of the Beast on their wall,
(just as we have the crucifix). I made a quick
decision; when I saw a sort of sling near-by.
I grabbed it and with all my strength
I hit their Emblem right in the eye (centre)
destroying it and all evil power within it.

59

Upon taking that decision I knew that that might cost me my life. But I thought it was worth it so long as I would destroy their power too. — As soon as I shattered it those followers of the beast accompanying me to their door were shaken with fright and trembled. And I understood that by destroying their Emblem they too were destroyed and had no power over me.

now, little one, be one with Me; let us continue to share; I am Lord, so do not fear; My Name: Jesus Christ, Son of God and Saviour ΙΧΘΥΣ

26. 12. 94

you have entrusted me with this Message. Committed me to take care of Your Interests, but my oppressors are joining

60

forces against Your Message to crush it. What can I do now with my bare hands?

I know; love Me and give yourself some rest; My child, I shall triumph in the end, so worry now about My Heartbeats; every Heartbeat is a call to a soul to return to Love; My Heartbeats are not all heard and, oh*, so many souls are heading into the eternal fires .... all I want from you is an unceasing prayer; be vigilant and use the discernment I

* this was a sigh.

61

have given you; have I not given you
enough proof of My Love?

Lord, give me please a visible sign of Your
Love.

flower-of-My-Passion, so be it; I shall
give you, for the sake of your love,
a sign of My Love, not that I have
not given you already, but I will
augment your perseverance with this sign
on you ♡

I love You to death.

ah.... how these words are a balm to Me

62

and in the mysteries of My Kingdom a salvation to a soul; come, My child!

27. 12. 94

My daughter, fragile as you are, can one say you were not witnessing in My Name? provided you remain weak and fragile, I will continue to overshadow you in My Strength; hear Me and rejoice: the One who has been feeding you and filling your mouth with Celestial Manna says to you: My Return is imminent, My Vassula, yes, rejoice and be glad!

63

I am on the road on which I had left; My Return is even nearer than it was when you were converted;* by the power of the Holy Spirit I have raised you, My child, to be in perfect union with Me and witness to the crowds in My Name giving yourself to them to the utmost of your capacity; your fidelity pleases Me; this is why I will continue to build My Plan in you until it is completed .... and the poor will hear

* That was 1985. (Today 9 years ago)

64

something never told before and will see
My Holy Countenance on you and those
who never knew Me will approach Me and
those whose eyes were veiled will see all
My glory .... whosoever will be moved by
My Spirit, who, today, blows everywhere,
will be heir to My Kingdom and
the Father will welcome him together with throngs of angels in Heaven;
I bless you now; ic

Excerpts from Notebook 76

7 January 95, NB p.1 . . . I Am Going In All Directions
Seeking By What Means I Could Save All Of You
- ✠ I will preserve the germ of a new generation
- ✠ Everyone will be called in front of My Throne to give an account
- ✠ My Forbearance is great but My Justice is just as great

12 January 95, NB p.12 . . . I Will Hasten My Plan
For The Sake Of This Remnant
- ✠ Stay awake...Soon, and that is your "soon," I will speak and My Voice will be of flame
- ✠ When there are some who despair, reassure them
- ✠ It will not be long now before My words will be fulfilled...I will judge fairly

13 January 95, NB p.16 . . . You Can Never Witness For Me
Without Being Persecuted

19 January 95, NB p.18 . . . Instead Of Fanning The Flame Of Love
I Am Offering To You All, Freely, Through These Messages...
So Many Of My Sacerdotal Souls Are Doing The Contrary
- ✠ The Night is almost here...and you are still so far from conversion
- ✠ You turned My Mysteries into a myth and your pastoral staff into a sceptre of falsehood
- ✠ You hasten to call what is divine and holy: "evil and a lie"
- ✠ How can you, who preach My Word daily not tell the times nor the signs?
- ✠ I will raise disciples in these End Times

28 January 95, NB p.37 . . . Give And Pass On...The Love, The Teachings
- ✠ Tell them that the God they have forgotten has never forgotten them
- ✠ Those who welcomed you in My Name have already My blessings

NB
76

1 February 95, NB p.38 (Croatia—Zagreb) . . . *Sow A Harvest Of Peace And You Will Inherit My Peace*
␈ Do not weep over material things
␈ If you only knew the message of peace I am offering you!
␈ Make peace with Me and be one in My Name

8 February 95, NB p.43 . . . *I Will Restore My Altars And Rebuild My Cities; Yet I Have To Discipline First*
␈ Is My Name to be profaned forever?
␈ As I reveal things beforehand I will reveal to you what My Right Hand will do
␈ I will adorn the remnant left with My Splendor and My Divinity
␈ What I am about to do grieves Me...what am I to do if no one listens?
␈ Father, I will, with compassion and tenderness, heal the wounds I will make by those same Hands that will strike

17 February 95, NB p.57 (Bangladesh) . . . *Never Have I Failed You*
␈ You, as My Echo, will be able to give My Celestial Manna to everyone
␈ I, Jesus, came to you in your poverty...to lift you to My Heart

18 February 95, NB p.60 (Dhaka) . . . *You Are Facing The Dawn Of The Great Events To Come...*
␈ This Inexhaustible Treasure revealed only to Gertrude, this Treasure that left her heart in total rapture...reserved for your times: the End of Times
␈ Now do you understand why the devil has you, My Vassula, as his prime concern and his prime target for destruction?
␈ Now I understand, Lord

1

3. 1. 95

Love is by your side ♡ you are weak
but in your weakness ♡ I am extolled ♡

ΙΧΘΥΣ ⊃⊂◦
Orthodox – Epiphany –   7. 1. 95

My God, Yahweh, Eternal Father,
    You who so patiently wait for our
conversion, come! Come and feed
all of us with Celestial Food to satisfy
our needs; You are known to have a
generous Hand, Righteous One, come and
save us! Turn the wicked man's heart
into a kind heart so that he too shall
assert Your greatness.

Yahweh my Tenderhearted Dad, the
    world does not yet know You entirely,
not the way You really are and only
with a demonstration of the power of
Your Holy Spirit shall mankind

2

realize the greatness of Your Name and extol
Your splendour of Your glory.

Yahweh, Father of each one of us, let
mankind learn Your acts of mercy,
tenderness and graciousness; remind them
Father, that the majestic glory of Your Kingdom
belongs to them too were they to have the
right heart.

I have passed on Your Words to every nation
You have sent me and I followed Your
command. I have, within my limits,
made Your Loving Portrait known to them
again, the way You revealed It to me,
so that they too rejoice and realize
that they are Your offspring and Your seed.
I followed Your instructions and reminded
them that they too are from royal descent.

Holy Father, as You are continuously
sending me out to proclaim Your Love
Hymn, by voice, as an echo, to share

3

Your Love Song with my brothers and sisters,
I pray for those who still are unaware
and living in a world of oblivion
and darkness, that Your Holy Spirit
may shine as a thousand suns in one in
their spirit. Yes, let Your Holy Spirit,
who outshines all the constellations put
together, turn every soul as an untarnished
mirror, an image of goodness, before
they disappear as though they had never
existed. Once restored, they too will go out
with zeal in perfect virtue, to proclaim
a visible image of Your Splendour and
Your Sovereignty, for they would have
acknowledged what is most divine.

Father, Source of Life, Fountain of Eternal
Life, Spouse, Your closeness to me
awakened every fibre of my wretched
heart, enabling me to penetrate into
Your mysteries and into Your inexhaustible riches. How could I be counted,
in my wretchedness, as one of Your

4

heiresses? Scarcely born I sinned and I
ceased to honour you, I sinned and I
ceased to be. The clay you had fashioned
had turned into your enemy. Your altar
had turned into a haunt of the lizard and
the spider, a mark of ill-disposition
and evil, clearly straying from the
Divine Truth. O feeble soul! with so
very little time to live on earth! what
had you become! The light of justice
was ready to strike my soul; Yet You,
in Your desire to free and to save were
far stronger than Death itself, the
powers of Darkness and Corruptibility,
and you flowed on me, Father, like a River,
healing what was considered fatally
wounded; raising what was taken for
dead and decaying.

And Your teaching, Lord, accompanied
Your visitations, already now are
exceeding the scope of my human
mind.

5

My Father,
  You are compassionate and
merciful, forbearing and forgiving,
  so do not avert Your Eyes from us,
  but lead us <u>all</u> back to You in the
  straight road.

daughter of My choice, I give you My
Peace.... I will grant your prayer, but
when My Love is rejected, what am I to
do? I am taking all means to save you
from the blazing fire and I am going
in all directions seeking by what means
I could save all of you;

  Your Holy Spirit is the Breath of Life:
He lifts us, revives us and graciously

6

makes us penetrate into Your mysteries.
   Your Holy Spirit turns us into live
and sacred Tabernacles, a Throne for
   the majesty of Your Son, a reflection
   of Your Image and into heirs for
   Your Kingdom.

   Father, allow now the heavens to tear open
                    this year
so that they pour out like never before Your
   Holy Spirit on us, then, we will all
      learn to love heavenly things and
   in Your Presence, we will rejoice.
      The dead bones will flourish and
   once again praise You adoring You.

ah*, My child, I am glad to hear your

eagerness considering your wretchedness;
   I will keep My Promise:

* A sigh

7

I will pour out My Spirit as never
before in history on all mankind to
deploy His power from one end of the
earth to the other, ordering a renewal
and a revival of My Sanctuary*....
yet, My Vassula, not everyone is worthy
of My Kingdom; My forbearance is
great but My Justice is just as great;
I will have to unleash before an
exhaling fiery breath, to restore Justice,
I will have to, My Vassula, destroy

* I understood it as: God's people.

8

the Beast and its followers by ejecting
from My Throne peals of thunder and
flashes of lightning to crush the godless and the empire of this world;
My justice will pursue all that does
not come from Me; I am mild in judgment, had I not been, none of you
today would be alive, I could have
destroyed you all at once; but, as you see
see how slow to anger I am? who
would then venture and say: " what have
you done to us? " when My sentence on

9

this earth Λ will pass? all these years Λ have been correcting you little by little and Λ have been giving you all the chance to repent, but so many of you from the beginning gave greater honours to dead things than My eternal glory; gold and silver* charmed you and you have taken a liking on these things excelling the honours due to Me ....
Λ shall protect though all those who will repent and Λ will preserve the germ

* God means : money

10

of a new generation for the ages to come;
lovers of evil and perverted mankind
will not go by unpunished .... everyone
will be called in front of My Throne to
give an account of the way they led
their life ♡

daughter♡, this short privation of
receiving messages* was so that you atone
for the sinners; endure pain*² without

*¹ God prevented me from being under dictation,
which in a way is my means of communication.
*² The wound on my right side.

11

complaining, I need acts of reparations,
I need generous souls, see how generous
My Son was with you? beforehand He
announced it to you*, so do not doubt
of His generosity ♡ come, allow Me to
use you to restore My broken altars;
I shall multiply My favours so long
as you look after My Interests and
My House; God - is - with - you, so
do not fear, I am with you; I am

* On the 26.12.94, Jesus said He would give
me a sign of His Passion on me.

12

bound to those who love Me ♡ come,
I bless you

α ☧ ω

12. 1. 95

Lord, let Your Voice be heard <u>this year</u>
as never before. How long Your people
are they to cry for help?

The Tradition You have passed on to us is
losing its hold. The Truth is blasphemed
daily and the apostate man gets the
better of the faithful. Surely You
see all this horror. How long,
Yahweh, are we to cry:
"Oppression!"
to the heavens, and You will not descend?
Our injury is grave and You are
the remedy, so, will You not let Your
Voice be heard
<u>this year</u>

13

most powerfully?

The apostates are already confiscating
Your Son's Sacrifice, are You
still not going to come and stop
their mischief? We are being slowly
stripped of our Salvation and
You my Lord, are You going to
remain silent?

We are ordered not to prophesy in Your
Name and are forced out of Your
House; we are expelled and dashed
upon, when we witness Your Love, to
keep silent. See? See what great
disorder they make out of Your Holy
Sanctuary? See how Your Spirit is
blasphemed daily?

14

When Jonah cried out, in his distress
to You, You answered him. When
from the belly of Sheol he cried
to You, You answered him and he
heard Your Voice. Today, my God,
has our lament not been heard yet?
Has it not reached Your Ears?

When Jonah was swallowed by the
fish he remained in the dark for
three days and three nights. What
about us, Lord? Are we to
remain in this darkness forever?

You are known to accord justice to
the poor in spirit and uphold the
good man's right, turn then Your
Eyes on our misery and save us!

My peace I give to you, My child,
hear Me and write: I will hasten

15

My Plan for the sake of this remnant,
so stay awake because you do not
know when I will be heard by flame...
and My Holy Spirit will be poured
out on many; when there are some
who despair, reassure them, reassure
them that their Father in heaven will
hasten His Plan. soon, and that is
your soon* I will speak and My Voice,
will be of flame destroying those who

* My soon is a human soon. God's soon
can easily pass 1000 years!

16

are destroying the earth*; be vigilant
and patient, it will not be long now
before My words will be fulfilled ♡
I will judge fairly;

A ☧ Ω

13.1.95

Lord, do You think I was slow to speak?
have I recited Your marvels as You
wanted me to? Jesus?

I Am; remnant, I give you My Peace!
sorrowful never be when a door is

* Ap. 11 : 18

17

shut in your face; I am with you,
so do not worry, My child; you can
never witness for Me without being
persecuted ♡ everything you do, even
though it might appear small and
not powerful, does not go in vain;
the trail you leave behind will be
marked and from thereon it is My
Work, so, little one, courage, I am
always with you .... so, this is how My
Father has favoured you ♡

What shall we do today?

18

pray, write and adore Me, nevertheless never neglecting your household duties, which have their charm too for Me; this is what I want from you; I will give you strength to be able to honour Me accomplishing all these things, so now let us write!

A Ω

19. 1. 95

peace be with you; fear not, beside you I Am; the 'Word' of God will be given to you this year again; your

19

generation is underestimating My Word*; some of you are even confiscating My Word; others are but too anxious to condemn whatever I say and they do not understand; in their wickedness they think wicked and are champions when it comes to destruction ♡ I tell you solemnly: Grace is offered to everyone today, but just like in My parable of

---

*It came as a complaint but severely at the same time. Like as if our Lord said: "What have you to say for this?"

20

the sower, they are this seed which fell
on the edge of the path; yes, they hear
My Word, but the devil comes and carries
away what they heard lest they believe and
be converted; then, becoming Satan's prey to
temptations, are eventually carried on the
way to destruction ♡ My Grace is upon
you, generation, but not for long now;
instead of fanning the flame of love I
am offering to you all, freely, through these
Messages and allowing My love to spread
and inflame each heart, so many of My

21

sacerdotal souls are doing the contrary;
Mercy is your hope of today but you
are content to fill your spirit with the
'knowledge' which is not knowledge at all
and reject My Mercy that I am granting
you today ♡ I am giving you signs
and wonders by the power of My
Holy Spirit am I giving you these prodigies,
I am raising the weak to testify on
My Glory and remind you that I
am thrice Holy! but there is no such
thing as peace in your heart, because

22

you have been rejecting My Holy Spirit,
the Carrier of Peace .... the Night is
almost here with you and you are so far
from conversion, generation! soon, and
that is your soon, when you will be
covered by your own blood, I, as Judge
then, will remind you of the blood
you were carrying on your hands for
having prohibited so many to receive My
graces through this Reminder of My Word,
you are as the Romans, crowning Me
with thorns daily; are you

23

going to say then as Pilate : " I am innocent of this blood " and wash your hands in perfumed water ? you refuse to accept the antidote to death, you refuse to acknowledge My Word given by My Holy Spirit in your days and take My Word instead frivolously; men of no faith at all ! you listen and listen without understanding, you see and see but cannot perceive My Glorious and Infinite Mercy I am shedding on you! ungrateful generation, you turned My testimony on

24

My Holy Spirit into a myth! you turned
My Mysteries into a myth and your
pastoral staff now has turned into a
sceptre of falsehood, so to whom shall I
compare you in your absolute nakedness?
to Cain? to Pharaoh? to the Pharisees?
or to Judas? you are stunned when I
brandish My Sword* before your eyes, unfaithful generation? did you not know
that the bearing of the sword has its
significance? have you not heard
that I am the warrior of

* It means the Word

25

Justice too* and not only of Peace? have you not read that I am The Faithful and True, the Amen, the Judge with Integrity, known by the Name: the Word of God*²? but it had been said that your era, Episcopal*³ of the Beast, will raise its sword against Me and My saints.*⁴

---

* Ap. 19: 11 And now I saw heaven open and a white horse appear; its rider was called Faithful and True; he is a judge with integrity, a warrior for justice!

*² Ap. 19: 13 He is known by the name, The Word of God.

*³ I understood that Episcopal was meant for the 2ⁿᵈ Beast, alias the False Prophet.

*⁴ Allusion to Ap. 19: 19

26

My Reign on earth is at your very doors, but you do not want it, no more than you want to hear My Word .... your wicked heart pays no attention to My warnings because you have renounced your humble shepherd's staff and preferred the sceptre of falshood, and when you hear The Word from My Mouth you do not warn your heart nor think of warning others, no, you see the Sword* coming but you pay no attention .... you object

* Sword is also for the Word of God.

27

and encourage others to do the same:
" all this is nonsense, pay no heed,
it is hysteria ; do not listen to this
frenzied lot ; do not listen to ' True
  Life in God ', invention of the Evil one ; "
you would say to reduce My Voice and
you hasten to call what is divine and
holy : ' evil and a lie ; ' bloodshed,
generation, will pursue you ; every ravine,
every hill, every sea, every mountain
will be struck down by My Sword ;
bloodshed will pursue you, because of

28

your sin and you shall die; but, if
however, even today you will renounce
your sin and repent with your heart
and promise to live in charity, union
and peace, you shall live and I
will recall your sins no more
come back to Me, generation, why are you
so anxious to die in your sin ?
come back to Me, renounce your sin
and you will live! have you not read: *
" I am the Amen: the Faithful and the

* Ap. 3:14

29

True Witness*[1], the Ultimate Source of
God's creation; true warrior for Justice?*[2]
how can you, who preach My Word
daily, not tell the times nor the signs?
you', who persist in declaring that I am
not the Author of this Message, I tell
you: you judge by human standards,
and you glory in your glory .....
beware, then, and keep your tongue
from judging; I am the sole Judge;

*[1] Ap. 19: 11
*[2] Ap. 19: 11

30

and you are indeed in My Hands ....
I have, with My Spirit, fortified what
was frail, so that through her,* My
Name will be praised and acclaimed in
every nation, so that the feeble man
finds his strength; I have commanded
you to be the Echo of My Word, a
scroll to be read, so that once they
hear and eat*2 they would joyfully take
courage to confess and repent;

* I understood that Christ was speaking
of me. *2 To eat the Word of God.

31

I have said in the Assembly of My saints:[*]
" I will deprive no one from My
Light; no one should remain imprisoned
in darkness; My Father is afflicted by
untimely grieving and the retribution He
has reserved for this faithless and apostatized
generation is at their very doors now; I
shall send in the chaos they are living
in, the Vessel,[*2] who carried Me in flesh

---

[*] Up in Heaven, Jesus assembled His saints
to declare to them His decision.
[*2] Our Blessed Mother

32

to carry this time again My Word, so
that I come to them like a drop of
morning dew in their desert; I will send
My Mother to teach them little by little
My ways and correct those who offend Me;
why, I Myself, shall descend too in
this desert to enliven the dead; Instruction and Wisdom shall be given freely
to them; We shall come with Our
Heart in Our Hand and offer it to them;
and like Two Lamps, standing side by
side We will shine on them ♡

33

I will not be slow in executing My Plan
and a time of Mercy will be granted to
them all; this is why, I will raise
disciples in these end of times to build
what lies now in ruin; I shall send
them to witness in My Name; I shall
send them where shrubs bear fruit that
never ripens and where the path of True
Knowledge is neglected; My precious ones*
will be sent in the entrails of this earth,
where sin is coiled up as a serpent in

* Those selected and sent out to testisfy e prophesy

34

its nest, to extirpate and uproot evil;
I shall send those ones to uproot the great
Plan of the Beast; I shall grant them in
their special mission the power and their
actions will be crowned with success; with My
Holy Spirit they will withstand fearsome
devils; with courage and perseverance they will
pay no heed to the stoning they will receive; My Holy Spirit will be their guide and
companion, guiding them prudently in their
undertakings; I will execute My promise
without delay and dispatch My Holy

35

Spirit from the Heavens to work with them
and teach them all that I have already
given them; I shall open their mouth
and fill it with My Word, and their
tongue will be like a sword. I will
guard My precious ones closely, from My enemies:* the oppressors, in those days; I will
save them from the traps set for them
and from the fatal hard stone aimed on
them; no, My all-powerful Hand will not
lack means of saving them; I will treat

*The apostates, followers of the Beast.

36

this generation leniently in spite of its wickedness;" – this is what I had said in My Assembly in Heaven ♡ today, although I have been speaking and pro- phesying through your mouth, the rich in spirit are not only oppressing Me, but are also blaspheming My Holy Spirit's Works; I tell you, the Day will come when you too will end up by admitting the truth of My Word!

daughter, although many join forces against you, I am with you, and your

37

Mother too; do not grow tired — remain
in Me so that the work I have given
you shines on all of you and all things ♡
   pray for unity, reconciliation and
the revival of My Church; be one in My
Name ♡

                                          28. 1. 95

Lord ?

I Am; lean on Me and trust Me, all
I ask from you in these days is to give
and pass on the Love, the teachings and
everything that I have given you, give!

38

speak! this is My Command, tell them:

blessed is he who has ears to hear
and eyes to see, theirs is the Kingdom of
Heaven; tell them that the God they
have forgotten has never forgotten them;

I, Jesus Christ bless each one of them;
those who welcomed you in My Name have
already My blessings ic

Croatia - Zagreb - 1.2.95

write: peace be with you; all day
long I have been with you and
have been stretching out My Hand to

39

you: " My people, My heritage, My seed,
turn to Me, make peace with Me;
make peace with Me....* I have loved
you from all eternity; return to Me and
I will return to you; sow a harvest
of love to obtain love; sow a harvest
of peace and you will inherit My Peace;
sow, blessed ones of My Soul, a
harvest of reconciliation and you will
obtain My Glory .... do not weep over

* These words sounded like a plea, Jesus
sounded as a beggar.

40

material things;* lift your eyes to heaven
and let your heart seek My Celestial
Laws so that through these My Kingdom
in Heaven comes in your hearts and My
Will be done in your hearts as it is
in the hearts of all the saints in Heaven;
— to this day I cry out as I once cried
out in Jerusalem: " if you only knew
the Message of Peace I am offering you

* Jesus Voice was raised when He said that,
  He said it as a command but at the
  same time as a reminder that nothing
  is important of this world, but one should
  search heavenly things.

41

still today, you would not fail to
seize it!" — but these things are
hidden from the learned and the wise
and are revealed to mere children; the
Kingdom of Heaven is revealed to the
simple and the humble; set your hearts
right and you shall have your reward
in the end ♡ and if you say: "what
can we offer You now?" I tell you:
"offer Me your heart, and I shall help
your lack of faith, open your heart
and I shall turn it into a heaven

42

for Me, your God, and in which I can
be glorified; come and eat from the
fruit I am offering you today while there is
still time; come to Me; your Master
is well on the road of return, this is why
I am telling you: make peace with
Me and be one in My Name; I bless
you all in My Name, leaving the Sigh
of My Love on your forehead. I χ θ Υ Σ

43

8.2.95

Who is there to have compassion on us
and grieve for us if it is not You?

We are still hoping for Peace, this Peace
Your Beloved Son has bequeathed us ...
  We have sinned against You and
against all the powers of Heaven.
  We have ceased to be, because
we have rejected Your Holy Name that
  is our identity: Source-of-Life.

  And now, this Great Revolt, this Apostasy
is eating Your House like cancer.

O my Yahweh! Brighter than a mil-
lion suns, how can man not notice
  Your brilliancy passing by them?
How can one say: "There is no proof
of Yahweh passing by. No sign is
  seen on His passing."

  God! You are like an arrow shot at
a mark, yet although they have

44

eyes they cannot see that the arrow has passed them by and is already on its target.

O our God, You are our Hope, come <u>now</u>, <u>this year</u>, without delay, to restore your broken altars and rebuild Your cities and Your House.

Ah Vassiliki! stop your sighing, I have heard you; My Hand is stronger than My enemy's; comfort shall be given to you soon, and I will redress My people and refresh your priests; I will restore My altars and rebuild My cities; yet, I have to discipline first the lawless who are

:45

champions when it comes to villainy ♡ they swallow apostasy as though ♡ they were eating the Bread of Life; even today, were they to repent I would show My favour and My pardon graciously to them, but I hear nothing from them ....
how can I abjure My fiery rage and retract My justice since this generation continues to give great honours to the devil? I am known to be good and forgiving and most loving but who today of these apostates invoke Me, calling Me: " my Father;

46

thus a tempest of fire soon will sweep away this iniquity and sin; <u>no one</u> of you knows that Day, and if any one says, he knows, he does not come from Me .... I will visit you in a time you least expect Me, an hour without a sign; suddenly, unexpectedly, you will be visited by a hurricane of a flame of devouring fire, what you are waiting for will come; I will speak and when I will speak, My Voice will melt the elements of the earth together with its iniquity and sin ♡ I love you

47

all with an everlasting love and My affection for you is beyond words, but is
My Name to be profaned forever? what I
am about to do grieves Me and overwhelms
Me with sorrow since I take no pleasure in
afflicting you; in My displeasure I will have
to redress you with fire; groan, daughter,
for the unrepentant; I shall accomplish
My intention and I shall carry out My
Plan till its end; as for those who did
not close their ear to My Voice and defen-
ded My Word, I tell you: do not grieve,

48

My Eyes see all, and I will judge each of you by what he does; as I reveal things beforehand I will reveal to you what My right Hand will do just after My Day,

My right Hand will lay the new foundations of earth and heaven, and once more I will adorn the remnant left with My Splendour and My Divinity; so, daughter, there is hope for your descendants; I am your Hope; I will make many return to Life, and will bear My Son's New Name on you; and you,

49

daughter, intercede for My House, take care of My Interests and I will take care of you; My Spirit has been given to you to apply My laws, to love justice and to bring My sons and daughters from far away; I have taught you and have given you a disciple's tongue to be My Echo and to put My Kingdom in their hearts; in your eyes, Paraskevi,* I have given you My light; in your soul I exhaled a perfume

* God called me with my second name which was given to me after a vow my mother made to our Saint Paraskevi, a saint for healing eyes.

50

of resurrection, I have breathed out a scent of myrrh, and in the tabernacle* of My Son, I have perfumed it with incense*²..... – and now, listen to your Father : *³

My Soul is overcome with grief but at the same time, by compassion; I have

* ¹ "The tabernacle of My Son", means, us, for when we receive Communion, Jesus enthrones Himself in us. We are all meant to be live tabernacles of Christ.

²* Incense drives Satan away. God had to perfume me with incense to purify me and receive His Son in the most perfect condition.

³* Suddenly God spoke very intimately and in a very paternal voice, just as any father who is filled with grief and wants to confide it to his child.

51

spoken, but very few listen, I knock* and
no one seems to hear, what am I to do
if no one listens? I have spoken Hope,
daughter, to all of you, yet when I speak
today which is the Hope you were all
longing for, My Word, no sooner given than
concealed, the seed of Hope I sow is
taken away and hidden .... I speak and
wait for a response, but My Word is
not heeded, yet, I am the Hope for
faithless hearts, but at the same time,

* "Knock" here is double sense : 'knock down', too.

52

the Sword that cuts hearts apart; so many hunger for My Word ....* but why do men conceal the treasures I am pouring out on them? if My Soul is overcome with grief it is because My Cup of Justice is brimming over now, overflowing on My Hands which are ready to strike and give a scourge to this faithless generation as never before, then, as I am Father, I will, with compassion and tenderness, heal the wounds I will make by

* Suddenly, God uttered that question as though speaking to Himself, alone, putting His thoughts openly.

53

those same Hands that will strike ....
this is the great Hope you are asking
Me for; I will come to bring everyone
home and heal their wounds; as I am
Father, I will attend My wounded children,
I will attend their needs, then they will
know that from the beginning they were
Mine and that <u>I Am who I Am is
Father and Lord</u>; I will bring their lips
to proclaim: " blessed is our Lord ;"
and once again they will proclaim the
Kingdom of Heaven; they will proclaim

54

it like never before because I will give them a new heart .... so do not be astonished when in these last days men are arrogant and betraying one another; do not be astonished by the multitude of false prophets rising and the propagation of errors and the distortion these false teachers do of Scriptures .... no, do not be astonished, My child, of men sneering now at you when you still say: " I believe in My Father in Heaven; I believe in one God, Father of all; I believe

55

in the glorious living Presence of His Beloved
Son in the Eucharist; I believe in Jesus
Christ, conceived by the Holy Spirit, born
of the Virgin Mary ;" no, daughter, they
do not believe in My Son's Resurrection
nor in His Divinity .... I tell you : be
in peace among fury and in tribulations
remain in My Peace; spread My Peace,
never allow your heart to be troubled
by the cruelty of men..... I am with you
even though you do not see Me, My
child, I am with you; My Son is well

56

on the way by which He left, to be
among you ♡ so courage! courage, and
do not be ♡ afraid; put your <u>hope</u> in
Me and no one else; I am Yahweh,
your Abba, and I promise you to bring
you home ♡ so, go and demonstrate
My Power ♡ and My Mercy; I am with
you: go, go and tell everyone:
" help comes from God, hope comes
from God; turn to Him and He
will save you. "
I bless you, Vassiliki, honour My

57

Name always!

Bangladesh   17. 2. 95

(Just before my meeting in Dhaka)

Lord? Uphold me and put Your words
constantly before my eyes! Remind me
of Your Teachings; O Lord, let Your
Words be before me as a Lamp
before my feet, not to stumble.

peace be with you; never have I failed
you and I never will; * Vassula, shshsh
listen to Me² .... lean on Me as you have
leaned before and I will guide you and

* I wanted to say something *² This was said very
                                                                  softly & gently.

58

through you others! we, us? ic

          Dhaka- Bangladesh -   17. 2. 95

(God brought me back to Bangladesh where
He first spoke to me. He brought me
in the premises of my conversion, and
where " True Life in God " began.)

My Vassula, I bless you; come, My Spirit
is with you and will be with you so
that you, as My Echo then will be able
to give My Celestial Manna to everyone;
My coming here again with you, was so
that I bless through you the premises of
the Nature of your being; by this I

59

mean, of your being in existence and alive! *

I, Jesus, came to you in your poverty,
in your misery, to lift you to My Heart
and make you the living sign of My
divine Mercy ♡ allow Me now to speak
through you and give My graces in these
meetings; reap with Me this rich harvest you have not prepared; pray without
ceasing and honour Me; keep Holy My
Name; I Jesus am with you ♡

IΧΘΥΣ

* Before my conversion I had ceased to be and
when God converted me I began to live.

60

Dhaka 18 . 2 . 95

Lord! You have educated me just like that.
Happiness Is reserved for the wretched
and the poor; this is how I came to
observe what the eye cannot observe unless
it is given us from above.

peace be with you; I could not see
the flower - of - My-Heart perish*; I could
not see you struck with blindness forever,
My Heart is your abode and your salvation;
how could I see this cloud overshadow-
ing My tent and remain silent? one

* In November 1985, when everything begun (True
Life in God), the angel Daniel, before introdu-
cing himself, took my hand and drew a
heart and from its middle a flower:

61

blow with My Breath was needed to blow

away what 'clouded My tent *'....

and now, one question: do you still

want to continue with all that 'I have

given you and evangelize with love for Love *²?

yes Lord.

say: " yes Lord, but with a fire inside

me, with zeal for Your House and Your

---

*   All this was said in metaphors. What
     Jesus means is as thus:
     The cloud : darkness of the soul, obscurity.
   Tent : my soul
   His Breath : The Holy Spirit
*²   My vows had to be renewed on the
     premises of the dawn of True Life in God.

62

Glory;" * renew then your vows of fidelity to Me ;² * and I then will renew
My graces ♡ upon you .... I will continue
to pour out My graces and My teachings
upon you; please Me and satisfy My
thirst, realize what I have given you;³ *
♡ My pleasure is to give ....
♡ remind your counsellor* how sacrifice
pleases Me, generosity is also agreeable in
My Eyes; I wish to remind both of

¹ * I said it   *⁴ Fr. O'Carroll
² * I did.   ³ * Jesus abruptly stopped and said
                            what follows!

63

you, how important it is to keep up
with My pace *¹, the urgency of My Message;
you are facing the dawn of the great
events to come; put your <u>heart</u> at
work; then, be gracious to one another;
tepidness in your work displeases Me; oh,
what could I have given you more that
I have not given you? I have given
you this <u>Inexhaustible Treasure</u> that
<u>was hidden from the eyes of mankind</u>
and was revealed only to Gertrude, *²

* Jesus 'step' is rather swift ....
*² It was revealed to her by St John the Evangelist

64

this Treasure that left her heart in total
rapture and her eyes captivated by the
wonder*; this Inexhaustible Treasure was
reserved for your times : the end of times;
My Sacred Heart treasured these riches
for your generation ; now, do you understand why the devil has you, My Vassula,
as his prime concern and his prime
target for destruction ?

    Now I understand Lord.

I will never fail you ;

* See note in the end.

Excerpts from Notebook 77

21 February 95, NB p.4 (Dhaka) . . . Strengthen My Church...

✠ And I will strengthen your faith and soul...Listen and your soul will live

✠ My company and My friendship will teach you with simplicity

23 February 95, NB p.9 (Dhaka) . . . Even A Mere Look At Me Rejoices Me

✠ My Sovereignty over you will transfigure your soul into a crystal-clear diamond, radiant and without blemish

25 February 95, NB p.11 (Indonesia) . . . Message For Indonesia

✠ Do not think that God is unapproachable

✠ Let your soul be at peace with Me the day I come to fetch it

26 February 95, NB p.16 (Indonesia) . . . I Am Who I Am Is Your Father

✠ You are not homeless; My Kingdom, My Splendour and the Truth are your home

✠ I...will fill your mouth from My Mouth with My Word...that gives light in your darkness

✠ My Mercy is Infinite, and My Compassion, too

27 February 95, NB p.20 (Indonesia) . . . Make Room Now For My Holy Spirit

✠ To dwell in you and continue to instruct you to live a True Life In Us

✠ Without these divine seeds your soul will remain a desert

✠ Do not be mystified by the action of My Holy Spirit

2 March 95, NB p.23 (Pully) . . . My Purpose Comes First

✠ From My Grace you are obtaining My Messages and My Will is that you go and announce them...to teach others

✠ Should anyone work for his self interests and without love, joy and self-giving, I shall intervene again

NB
77

3 March 95, NB p.28 . . . Have Me As First
- ✠ I am your Friend and I observe you with love and compassion
- ✠ Treat Me tenderly by answering My Calls with zeal and wholeheartedly

6 March 95, NB p.31 . . . Do Not Lose Heart, Daughter
- ✠ In time of death I will save you
- ✠ Humiliation and calumny sanctify you
- ✠ My Knowledge is sweet, but also sour...sour because of this painful apostasy of My Church

18 March 95, NB p.41 . . . My Plan Is To Save You All
- ✠ A throng of angels will...accompany you in your mission

21 March 95, NB p.44 . . . This Inexhaustible Treasure...Kept Hidden For Your Times, When People's Hearts Would Grow Cold
- ✠ Ice does not endure the fire

30 March 95, NB p.47 (Japan) . . . I Will Betroth This Nation Message For Japan
- ✠ My Name is Jesus...Soon I shall come with myriads of angels...I am the only Truth and your Way to Heaven
- ✠ Come to Me as you are...do not say, My beloved Japan: "I cannot speak, and if I do, He will not hear me" I am at your doorstep now

31 March 95, NB p.53 (Japan) . . . I Have Decided To Hurry Up My Return
- ✠ The rest of My Messages will be given to you promptly before the day of the Antichrist's appearance
- ✠ ...this silence will be broken...upon opening the Sixth Seal
- ✠ My enemies will tremble and beat their breasts

I

work with Me*[1] and please Me; I am your life .... pray, that the Evil one does not venture too close to your union*[2] .... pray for the completion of your work; pray and ask the Father to make you perfect; I, Jesus, bless both of you and remember: confide in one another, bless one another, be an example of what unity will be like! be one ♡   ΙΧΘΥΣ   ⟨fish symbol⟩

Note: Saint Gertrude is often called the Great, as she was one of the greatest mystics of the Catholic Church. Though she lived

* Jesus smiled. *[2] Fr. O'Carroll's and mine.

2

nearly four centuries before St. Margaret Mary,
she had a great devotion to the 'Heart of
Jesus. Her book " The Herald of Divine
Tenderness " is a living poem on Divine
Love, a love always linked to the Sacred
Heart.

One of the most famous of all her visions
concerned the Heart of Christ. The vision took
place on the Feast of St. John the Evangelist.
In her book she speaks of herself in the
third person.

A reading from St. Gertrude:

" Whilst she was, as was her wont, wholly
absorbed in prayer, the disciple whom
Jesus loved so well, and who for that
reason should be loved by all, appeared
to her. She then said to him : " And
what grace can I obtain, wretched me,
on your feast day ? " He answered :
" Come with me, you are the chosen
one of my Lord; let us rest

3

on His breast in which are hidden all
the treasures of blessedness."

– Then he took her to our Lord and both
placed themselves on our Lord's Heart.

That is where she discovered this Inexhaustible
Treasure He was hiding in His Heart. When
she asked the Evangelist why wasn't this
treasure given before or why hadn't
the Evangelist spoken of this Treasure,
St. John said:

"My mission was to deliver to the Church,
in her first age, a simple word on the
uncreated Word of God the Father that
would afford the whole of humanity
enough to contemplate until the end
of the world, yet without any person
ever succeeding in fully grasping it.

But to tell of the pulsations of the Heart
of Jesus has been reserved for modern

4

times so that, in hearing of these things,
the world already old and growing cold
in the love of God, may be rekindled
and grow warm again. "
(St Gertrude 1257 - 1302)
(Legatus Divinae Pietatis, Bk. IV, ch. IV)

Dhaka 21. 2. 95

peace in your heart; Vassula - of - My - Sacred
Heart, Flower - of - My - Passion, Offspring -
of - My - Father, I want you to be perfect;

Lord, where shall I find sufficient
words to glorify You? You have honoured
my wretchedness with Your stupendous
awe - inspiring Presence.
Since then no task was too hard for me,
with Your Presence everything became easy
and a delight.
You taught me that in Your

5

right Hand You hold the Victory, and
  that Death was swallowed up by Life.
O Saviour so anxious to save and
  fortify, Your graciousness visited me
at night, in the night of my heart, to
  sing a Festival, rousing a corpse.
        You put all Your Heart into
Your song out of love for all of us;
  and out of me You made a Harp
before Your Altar ....

  Let the music sound for our King,
      let it sound !
  Let the music flow to the ends of
        the earth and vibrate on every
ravine, every mountain, and valley!

praise My Name always, like now! so
that your only Love rejoices. Vassula,
strengthen My Church and I will strengthen

6

your faith and soul; the little you give to Me pleases Me, the greater you give to Me delights Me! My Father never fails you, He always comes to your rescue[*]; I am always with you ....

Do not forget that I am dust and that with one gust of wind I am gone. The Waters from Your Breast are cascading over the moun-

[*] I had noticed this myself too. God the Father rushes first to console me. — One day, under very heavy persecution, I went on my knees crying for help to Jesus, I wrote my complaint (using my charism) and instead of Jesus responding, God the Father rushed to me and consoled me promising that the next day 'it will be arranged': His word came to realization as He had said. — I know the Father has a weakness for me but so have I for Him.

7

tains and into the valleys*; You are supplying
water for all those who are thirsty,
and You are sending me across the
hills to all nations to cry out:

" From God alone come victory and
strength." Do not crouch out of
thirst anymore, stir your memories
and recollect yourselves, all you who
lie in the dust, for your Dew is not
beyond reach. You have forgotten
who made you, but if you drink,
your memory will be restored! *²

" Oh come to the water all you who are
thirsty ; though you have no money,
come! ...." (Is. 55:1)

and I will say : listen, and your soul

* An outpour of the Holy Spirit.
*² Jesus helped me with His Spirit to write
what I have written.

8

will live ....

And now my Saviour, You who count first in my life, forgive my wretchedness and my failures.

beloved, I love you anyway;

Dissolve the mist around me, Inexhaustible Treasure, Thrice-Holy, Starlight of my Night, Vessel of my soul, Pillar of blazing Fire do not leave me imprisoned In darkness; Clap of Thunder* revive my soul and grant me Instruction and Correction.

♡ My company and My friendship will
♡ teach you with simplicity, take My Hand and together we will continue

---

* God's Voice is like a clap of thunder: (Jn 12: 28-29) "A voice came from heaven,' I have glorified it, and I will glorify it again': People standing by, who heard this, said it was a clap of thunder.

9

on the road I have prepared for you, so that I bring you to perfection ♡

Dhaka - 23. 2. 95

(I was looking at Christ's portrait)

Author of Beauty how can one not be charmed by you? Wretched as we are and only capable of destruction, Your love for us never fails. We sin, yet we are still yours, giving us instructions that although we are blotched with sin, You, in your ardent desire to grant us Your pardon, will continue to pursue us as a Lover pursues his betrothed : to conquer us entirely.

yes! what will I not do for all of you to conquer your heart entirely! so little is needed for your Saviour to make Him

10

happy; even a mere look at Me* rejoices Me; I can make you Mine forever and My Sovereignty over you will transfigure your soul into a crystal-clear diamond, radiant and without blemish; I tell you solemnly, unless you die to your "you", you will not acquire eternal life ♡ I am the light of life; and you, daughter, remember: your brothers and sisters are still far from My Divine Heart which can

---

* That is when I had looked at His Portrait with love.

II

render them divine, they are on their
way to perdition and Destruction is gnawing
on them without them even realizing it!
creation! you have only to will, and
I shall descend upon you like a River,
that ever-flowing Source coming from My
Breast ♡ ic

Indonesia - Jakarta 25. 2. 95

My Lord, Your Word burns our heart like
fire, so how is it that when You speak
their* heart does not burn?

pray for these, that I may give them a

* The persecutors of these messages.

12

heart to acknowledge Me 🤍 blessed one of My Soul, accept this painful exile on earth;* one day I will show you its outcome; today I have brought you here to Indonesia, as much as I have brought together in one assembly all of you. tell them: do not think that God is unapproachable, God is near you and loves you ... honour His Name; return to Me and change your lives and live holy for Holy is My Name; allow Me to redress you, for

* To have seen the Lord, you want to be with the Lord.

13

this I need your total abandonment; your only Refuge is My Heart; listen and understand: I have said that all flesh is like grass and its beauty like the wild flowers of the fields, but the grass withers and the flowers fade, but My Word remains forever .... and your soul will keep on living; let your soul be in peace with Me the day I will come to fetch it; so that you inherit My Glory; do not deceive yourselves now and say: " soul, you have plenty of things now, take things as they come:

14

have a good time and roll in your wealth,
obviously the inheritance is yours;" realize,
My child, the wilderness you made of your
soul; realize, My child,* how painful it is
for Me to see your drought; I have always
loved you with an everlasting Love; diminish My pain, efface My pain and return to
Me, your Father, your Creator, your Saviour
and your Life ♡ pray from your heart,
and I shall hear you; forgiveness is given to
you, if you ask it! Indonesia,

* The Lord is speaking to each one.

15

direct your steps into My Steps for My Day
is near and when I come, I shall come
with Fire so allow Me to find you fit for
My Kingdom .... ask for My blessings and
I shall give them to you; which father
refuses the well-being of his child? so
how much more would I, who am the
Source of Love, <u>give</u> to anyone who asks!
I am near you, daughters and sons, and
I bless you offering to you My Peace; come
and acknowledge your sins, facing Me,
and I will respond to your cry of repentance;

16

Vassula, I am Yahweh, your beloved Father and Father of all; praise Me and follow Me without delay, up now and pray the Our Father the way I honoured you by teaching it to you; I love you tenderly!

A ☧ Ω

Indonesia   26. 2. 95

With my lips, Lord Almighty, I have repeated Your words that I heard coming from Your own Mouth, to many nations, so that they too enjoy Your Presence and rejoice in Your Law. Let me not forget or neglect Your Word and do not allow me to stray from Your Commandments, revive my soul with Your Word, my Lord.

17

I give you My Peace; My child, you are not Fatherless; I Am who I Am _is_ your Father; you are not homeless, My Kingdom, My Splendour and the Truth are your home; you are not restrained from food, for I, with My Own Hand fill your mouth from My Mouth with My Word; sceptres and thrones can never be esteemed more than My Word; to what can you compare My Riches? My Vassula, you were once starved for My Word and My Heart, this Heart of the most tender of

18

fathers was in mourning, and filled up with
sorrow and pity; how many more are like
you were once* ! and how many more
will I have to resurrect then nourish.... but
it was said that in these last days My
creation would fall into such an apostasy
and coldness of heart that many, even
though they would not reject Me, would
be affected; it has been said that
Satan would increase in power in your
days; but My Mercy is Infinite and My

* Spiritually dead.

19

Compassion too; if the curse comes out of
Satan's mouth, a blessing from My
Mouth overpowers his curse; My blessing is
the Word from My Mouth that gives light
in your darkness and on those who live
in the shadow of death; My favour is
upon you and so everything I do in these
days is for the salvation of your generation; and you, daughter, present Me in
your meetings as you have always done;
embellish My House and I shall embellish
yours;*   vivify My House as I
    * God means my soul

20

vivified yours*; caress Me your Father with your love; let us work;

A ☧ Ω

Indonesia 27. 2. 95

I am still mystified by Your choice, my Lord, and all that is happening to me!

do not be!*[2] I am Lord of the heavens and earth; I tell you, out of a Nothing I can make an Altar on which all My Treasures can be laid .... tell Me: by what means did you obtain all the Knowledge, strength and zeal to evangelize?

* Vivified me spiritually *[2] This came like a command.

21

By Your Holy Spirit, my Lord.

yes! by the power of My Holy Spirit ♡
make room now for My Holy Spirit
to sow in you seeds from Heaven, allow
My Holy Spirit to cultivate your soil and
make a terrestrial Eden in you; allow, My
beloved one, My Holy Spirit to burn all
the dry plants in you and replace them
with Celestial seedlings and young vineyards;
allow My Holy Spirit to turn your soul into
another Paradise where We* would feel We

* The Holy Trinity

22

are surrounded by humility, peace , love,
and joy; *¹ yes, allow My Holy Spirit to
take root in the middle of your soul and turn
it into another Paradise ; so make room now
for My Holy Spirit to dwell in you and
continue to instruct you to live a <u>True</u>
<u>Life in Us</u>²*; say now these words :

                    Lord,

    give us Your Kingdom, so that we
        may obtain incorruptibility and the
            deity to have eternal life; Amen;

* The seeds and seedlings of Paradise² * The Holy Trinity.

23

learn that only the seeds sown by My Holy Spirit in you can yield fruits in abundance; without these divine seeds your soul will remain a desert, uncultivated and a land of drought! so, daughter, do not be mystified by the action of My Holy Spirit .... come, My pupil, evangelize in My Assemblies ♡ ic

Pully.   2. 3. 95

My Lord?

I Am; peace be with you; till now I have put up with you and all the delay

24

due to administration *.... I want to untangle you from these things that take up My time! I am telling you: I am the One who enlisted you to write down My Messages; you will not keep up with My time were you to continue the way you do now; I have given you certain rules and again they were not followed; from

* Christ was reproaching me that the messages He dictated to me were "put aside", and I had taken up His time of dictation for administration, e.g. fixing my travelling programme faxes non stop, and people keeping me on the phone.

25

My Grace you are obtaining My Messages
and My Will is that you go and announce
them as you do in public, to be able to
teach others; — I shall put a new heart
in you and give it a spark and with My
Grace you will comply with My rules; pray
and be with Me in My Calls; I have put
up with you so far; from now on My
purpose comes first; from now on you will
answer My Calls and not those of others;
My Messages come first; from now on you
will spend your time with Me in

26

harmony* and not with the great demands that so many impose on you, nor will you spend your time with discussions on the telephone; tell people who would like to hear " the latest novelty " of My Messages to recollect themselves in prayer and equip themselves with what I already have given them; Vassula, remind everyone who works for True Life in God that I have chosen them, yet if anyone fails Me I

---

* When I am under dictation with our Lord I feel happy and peaceful. But the administration work, etc. put me in stress and I had lost my peace, because I was "pushed" by people to hung on what they wanted from me. I ended up working for others e not for J∅

27

am free to replace him; I desire that
each one of them re-examine his conscience
and: pray to obtain an opening; try to
discover what is missing and what I want
out of you; Satan is observing all of you
and has sworn to stop My Plan by
obstructing it and by using strong opposition; his threats are reaching heaven
daily; without delay work hard and willingly; for My sake work with My
Spirit and not with yours; — should
anyone work for his self-interests and

28

without love, joy and self-giving, I shall intervene again .... and you, daughter, from now on be careful and on your guard; Wisdom will continue to teach you, so, <u>no more</u>! * — rely on Me completely, and continue with the gift of prophecy that I have given you; I am with you;   ic

3. 3. 95

My Lord?

I Am; peace be with you, My child;

---

* This came very strongly, it sounded as one says BASTA! in Italian. I understood that Jesus does not want me to do 'paper-work' even if it is for True Life in God, nor delaying on phone-calls.

29

hear Me: in your nothingness I can work marvels, so adapt yourself to My regulations and never forget how I work; keep Me in your heart and you will obtain My Peace; never forget what I have told you yesterday! have Me as first and give Me some of your time to continue writing My Messages; please Me and en-grave My Name on your heart; I am your Spouse and My Name should be honoured; let everyone around you who work too for My Love Hymn behave

30

towards you as if you were not anymore among them*; the fruit of your labour should multiply in their hands*²; I Jesus am with you; place Me, My Vassula, before and above all in the world so that your exile will not appear to you as hard as now; hurry up, My child, and understand how precious and how dear you are to Me; I am your Friend and I observe you with love and compassion; I shall

---

* That means: to start taking initiatives.

²* I understood: the writtings of True Life in God, and the meetings I held testifying.

31

never fail you; treat Me tenderly by answering My Calls with zeal and wholeheartedly, I love you Vassula and I., I will
never abandon you; I shall fortify
you City-of-Mine with My Spirit
come now and make the sign of My
Cross on you ....* good; come now

I X Θ Y Σ

6. 3. 95

(Suddenly the Cross on me became too
heavy.) In the beginning my Lord, You
cuddled me and watched each breath of
mine with a motherly tenderness.

* I signed myself with a cross.

32

You modelled me, remember, as soft
   clay is modelled with so much care,
never have I felt that I was being felled
   so that I can start my life again; so
tender was Your touch;

You then endowed me with Your Holy Spirit,
   the Life-Giver, and my days since
then ran hurrying by, seeing only delight
   in their flight;

Why am I today trodden by the insensitive
   who cannot peer through their shadowed
darkness?
They who live under an impenetrable veil
   and who have to grope their way
when they have to walk?

You promised me that their greatness
   will be brought to nothing and their
wisdom to dust.

   You are known to save those of

33

downcast eyes and the innocent, You
are known to take note of everything
said and done; am I to be constantly crushed beneath the Rubble?*

How much more can I be struck? Has
my staggering not challenged You yet?
Can I become more abject than I am already?

And now You delight to have me where
light itself is like the dead of night.

listen My lamb: to tell you now that
I will unburden* you from My Cross, you

---

¹* The Rubble: the spiritually dead.
²* The word unburden here has a double sense.
a) Relieve b) Burden also means 'an oracle,'
in Hebrew: "Massa". The double meaning here
is: " to tell you now that I will stop giving
you oracles," etc. thus the word: Un burden
Read: Jr 23: 33 – 40

34

so generously asked Me to share with Me would
be complete folly on My part! the trials
you are bearing for Me are not more than
anyone has .... do not lose heart, daughter.
and do not venture to say: " has He
who assesses the heart no understanding ? "
My Wisdom cannot be explored by men;
look ! your race is not over, after all
have you not heard with what desperation
the prisoners of Hades*[1] knock on your door*[2]?

*[1] Purgatory.
*[2] Several times between 4.00 - 4.30 a.m the door to my
bedroom was nearly dashed down from the souls' knocks.

35

have I not schooled you so that your heart understands your mission? Vassula! have you not heard their groans? tormented in the night, those souls dash at your door for help*; you are feeble and you waver now ..... do not disappoint Me ..... in time of famine I came to you to nourish you and again in time of death I will save you, so make Me happy and allow Me to use you for My Interests; love Me and let your love for Me augment so that

* Help to them is given by prayers.

36

vermin will never cover your flesh; augment
your prayers and offer them for My intentions;
I will never hide My Face from you; never; *
Fruit-of-My-Love, Flower-of-My-Thorned-
Crown, Blossom-of-My-Church, do not
be intimidated by My Nails; Pupil-of-My-
Council, do you not know that humiliation
and calumny sanctify you? have you forgotten that I have counted you as one of
My daughters of My Church? what is more
desirable than being kin to My Blood?

* Jesus said these words very solemnly.

37

I Myself have chosen you to be My mouthpiece over many nations and teach you the
Sacred Writings* by dropping in your mouth
My Knowledge like honey that drips from
the comb; My Knowledge is sweet, but also
sour*; sweet, because I am announcing My
glorious triumph with My people, and
sour, because of this painful apostasy of
My Church preceding My victory ♡ ....
ahh* generation! the hour of darkness is

---

*¹ The Holy Bible
*² Allusion to Ap. 10 : 8 - 11 *³ This was a deep sorrowful
                                              sigh from our Lord.

38

upon you now that you have embarked into the 'boat of death', it will lead you to
death; the danger signal was given to you
now close to ten years*¹; it had been echoing
in your ear close to ten years, but you were
fleeing from My Voice thundering all this
while .... foreigners have been more attentive
and sensitive to My Voice than you, you*²
who call My Name daily and raise Me daily;

* ¹ This message will inaugurate its 10ᵗʰ anniversary
in November 1995.
* ² I understood: the sacerdotals .. Many refuse to
believe in the prophetic charisms that could help
the Church and in fact become persecutors to the Holy Spirit
who gives such charisms.

39

if only you could listen, if only you who are dying would see My saving help¹! but a veil of shadow hangs over your eyes .... ah *, if you only knew how utterly dead you are and how the rest of you have become grave-diggers for your own graves .... to bear witness against My Holy Spirit and to try to conceal My Works that are for My Glory will lead you into eternal fires; I tell you, daughter, there is no fathom to My sorrow, so allow Me,

* Another deep sigh

40

daughter, to share My Cross with you, and allow Me to continue to cultivate you till the end ♡ turn your eyes to Me and never leave Me ♡ from your sight; I promise you that I will accomplish your mission together with you; avoid any tendency to administration, for such has been the true cause of this perilous delay! make My Message known to everyone and show them that I am a God who saves ♡ IΧΘΥΣ ⤳

41

Paris   18. 3. 95

(The delay of 6 months work for His Messages
was caught up in 2 weeks. I wrote for 2 weeks
non-stop, 7-9 hours a day. I left all the administration that ate up 'all Jesus' time and
obeyed Him by doing only the writings. Telephones
too were stopped short. Letters were unopened
and sent to the association to deal with. Prog-
rammes for meetings were not done by me any more,
but by the association of True Life in God, in France.)

Vassula, your efforts please Me; alone you

are not; secondly, I delight when My words

of correction are not taken lightly nor go by

unheeded; allow Me to be your guide and

your spiritual director; I have established My

Salvation Plan in you so that through

you My Messages will be accomplished by

42

My Will ♡ allow Me to use you now only for a little while longer; persevere at your duty and enjoy doing it; My company to you is the sweetest of the sweet; if thorns and briars come, do not fear, these have to come anyway, I will lift you to go over them; they shall not harm you. — enlarge My Vineyard, daughter, and I will extend all the fruits of My Vineyard and its boundary will have no end; — My Plan is to save you all, but I need generosity to atone the guilt of this

43

generation; great is My sorrow to watch them going in the fire prepared by My Enemy; * I Am the Source of Life! and from My Breast, Living Waters flow out! come! come and drink, I will not charge you, if any man is thirsty, let him come to Me! I am the Life and before you and among you all, I stand ....

— daughter, a throng of angels will be by your side to accompany you* in your mission,

---

* Suddenly Jesus cried out with a loud Voice.
2* In my meeting in Paris at the ' Palais des Congrés

44

I, Jesus, bless you and tell you:
'lo tedhal !' *¹

IΧΘΥΣ

21. 3 . 95

Blessed be Your Name, who has blessed me thrice,
allowing me to see His hidden plan that
was in His Sacred Heart from the beginning
and that was revealed to His chosen one
He so well loved *².   Now, me too, in Him have
I heard His message, this Inexhaustible Treasure
of which St. Gertrude had a glimpse.
Soon there will come a time where there
will be no further need for neighbour to try
to teach neighbour, or brother to say
to brother, 'learn to know the Lord'.
No, they will all know You, the least no
less than the greatest, since

* 'Do not fear!' in Aramaic, Jesus' Language.
*² St. John the Evangelist

45

— You will forgive their iniquities and
    never call their sins to mind." (Heb. 8:11-12)

I shall try to walk in the path You laid out
for me without swerving and cherish the
Treasure You have given us all.

I am well pleased with your work;* draw
from My Heart this Inexhaustible Treasure
which I kept hidden for your times, when
people's hearts would grow cold, ungrateful,
full of boasting and irreligious ♥ My intentions
are to rekindle this dying flame and
make them change their mind so that

* The delay was caught up.

46

once healed they would acknowledge Me as
the Supreme High Priest, the Christ, and
the King of kings ♡ come then close to
Me and enjoy what good things you see,
take your fill from this Inexhaustible
Source of well-being; do not be discouraged
when people look on, uncomprehending
that Grace and Mercy is among them,
pray for these; ice does not endure the
fire; I will melt this ice with My
Holy Spirit, so rely on Me and say:

47

"God is with us soon;"

I X Θ Y Σ ⊂⊃ your Beloved

Tokyo-Japan - 30.3.95

My Lord? Look down from Heaven, from your holy and glorious dwelling. Here I am among Your children, yet so many of them do not know You, as a most compassionate Father.

Father, make Your Name known, let Your Spirit guide your children since You are our Father.

Open now the heavens and come to us. At Your Presence, all the nation, will be moved and will give up the power of sin that holds them.

At Your Presence, this nation too will be betrothed to You

48

and will be called:

" The Betrothed. "

yes! I will betroth this nation to Myself, with tenderness and love will
I betroth them, and in the end
with one mouth they will proclaim
with delight My Name:

" our Father! "

then the whole land will be wedded
to Me ...." and as the bridegroom rejoices
in his bride, so will I rejoice in them *"

* Is: 62: 5   A ☧ Ω

49

Later on, Jesus spoke:

pray for My children of Japan; write
this and tell them:

I am in your days, these days of
darkness, revealing to you all My Holy
Face; I have not come to remind
you of My Presence so that I condemn
you, I have come to call all of you
to My Sacred Heart! I intend to
give sight to the blind and take away
the sight of those who say they see ♡
I shall choose weakness to show My
Power and Poverty to show My Riches and

50

My Glory; open your hearts and speak to Me; My Name is : Jesus, and Jesus means : 'Saviour';

soon, very soon I shall come with myriads of angels, yes, My Return is imminent; look around you, have you not noticed My Signs? do not be afraid of Me, I am the only Truth and your Way to Heaven; come to Me as you are, do not wait to be saints, do not say, My beloved Japan: " I cannot speak ", and if I do, He

51

will not hear Me;" I am standing at your doorstep now, with My Heart in My Hand to offer it to you ♡ I am the Sacred Heart and I have made a New Hymn of Love for all of you; Mercy descends now to call all those who never sought Me nor ever knew Me to join in the assembly of My saints too ♡ Scriptures say: "God does not have favourites, but that anybody of any nationality who fears God and does what is right is acceptable to Him;" *

* Acts 10: 34-35

52

did you not know that I am a God
who is meek and gentle, forgiving and
full of pity? your unworthiness attracts
Me for I am Everything and I can
look after you; your incapacity to
reach Me makes Me eager to lean from
Heaven to lift you to Me; allow Me then
to enter your heart and I shall adorn
you with My glory! seek Me and you
shall find Me, knock and I shall
open to you; even if you say: "who
am I to step into Your Heart?"

53

I will tell you: " you are My child, My Own and My Seed; you belong to Me and to no one else; you come from Me and from no one else; this is why I want you in My Heart; " — no, perhaps you have not sought Me but I have found you; this, Japan My child, is My Message for you; I bless you, leaving the Sigh of My Love on your forehead; IXθYΣ ><>

Oita - Japan 31. 3. 95

When I was imprisoned in darkness and kept

54

captive in the dungeon of sin, where grim
faced spectres haunted my soul, and
while I thought I would remain there,
forgotten and banished from Your Eternal
Light, You, like a thousand brightly
blazing suns descended from Your
Glory illuminating my dreadful night;
Suddenly, someone was standing
there and my heart leaped with hope;
A Breath slid over my face
opening my eyes: and the Invisible
God became Visible; and while I
was standing face to face with Purity,
Splendour and Sovereignty, I came
to be; The Breath of Omnipotence
raised me and my Lawlessness ceased
to be.

dust and ashes, I have given you a heart
of flesh now and inspired in you a
living spirit; although your mind

55

had sunk into deep forgetfulness, My
Mercy came to your help and rescued you,
curing you. I said: "I shall become her Spouse, her Educator and her
Protector and she will be My bride, My
pupil and My child, and I will
lead her by a marvellous road; her
feet will tread on sapphires; I shall be
her starlight while crossing gloomy valleys
and her rod and staff when
persecuted and hunted; though she will
be crossing deserts and valleys, she will

56

never thirst or hunger, I will be her Cup and My Body will be her food; I shall be the theme of her praises and her Song in My assemblies;" and now, child of My predilection, courage, your race is not over, but I shall finish it with you, My Hand upon your hand*; be in Peace and allow Me to instruct you every day! I instructed My disciples and formed them and like I have nourished them

* Double meaning: Helps me to write and walk.

57

with My Word, so will the One who raised you nourish you; with My Holy Spirit I will teach you to avoid all evil; do you still want to learn from Me?

Yes, Lord.

good; then you shall learn ♡ the Father and I will continue ♡ to pour on you Instructions like prophecy .... My pleasure is to teach, particularly souls like yourself who must depend on Me only, and are well-disposed, eager like children

58

who want to please their Teacher! I
delight in such souls ♡ finally, I want
to add one more thing on account of
My Messages: I have decided to hurry
up with My Return; I will not wait too
long to return to you; even though many
are refusing to believe this, they will
believe when it happens but then their
heart would be unprepared to receive Me;
My Return is imminent and this is why,
daughter, I was anxious for you to
hurry up and complete the work. My

59

Father and I gave you through My Holy
Spirit; My Treasure, allow Me to continue
My dictation without any delay on your
part; My affection for you is great
and I will help you to put your heart
right and please Me ♡ see? see how I
unburdened you from the administration work?
now I will have you just for Myself;
I will call and you will be available;
the rest of My Messages now will be given
to you promptly before the day of the
Antichrist's appearance .....

60

How are we to continue when he appears?

for just over three days and three nights *[1+2]
you shall not be able to continue as you
want; but this silence will be broken by
My Own Hand upon opening the sixth
seal; *[2] rejoice, for I shall be with you
soon! My Voice will be heard and My
enemies will tremble and beat their
breasts *[3] ♡ I am today suffering with you
just as ♡ I agonized in Gethsemane; come

*[1] Symbolic number for 3½ years.
*[2+3] Look at 'noks', end of message.

61

Vassula, I bless you for giving Me honour and praise* and for giving Me your time to write through your hand; ΙΧΘΥΣ 🐟

Notes for the reader to understand.

'For just over three days.' Ap. 11:11. "After the three-and-a-half days, God breathed life into them and they stood up ..."

This regards the two witnesses, the two prophets. Elijah and Moses. The Two Hearts today, the Immaculate Heart of Mary and the Sacred Heart are prophesying to us in a parallel ministry of Elijah and Moses. Elijah represents prophecy and the preparation of the Lord's coming, as John the Baptist who had come in the same spirit as Elijah. Moses represents the Law.

* Jesus means during my meeting.

62

The three - and - a - half days, all heavenly
prophecy will be silenced, which will be the
time of the reign of the Antichrist.
    'A time and two times and a half a
time ; and all these things are going to
happen when he who crushes the power
of the holy people meets his end." Dn. 12:7

" The beast that comes out of the Abyss is
going to make war on them and overcome
them and kill them." Ap. 11:7

" Men out of every people, race, Language
and nation will stare at their corpses,
for three - and - a - half days, not letting
them to be buried, and the people
of the world will be glad about it and
celebrate the event by giving presents to
each other, because these two prophets
have been a plague to the people of
the world." Ap. 11:9-10

63

" But this silence will be broken by My Own
Hand upon opening the sixth seal. "
     This will be the end of those three
and a half years of the Antichrist's power.

" After the three-and-a half days, God
breathed life into them and they stood up,
and everybody who saw it happen was
terrified;   then they heard a loud voice
from heaven say to them, ' come up here';
and while their enemies were watching,
they went up to heaven in a cloud .
Immediately , there was a violent earthquake
and a   tenth of the city collapsed;
seven thousand persons (that is a great
number of all classes) were killed in
the earthquake, and the survivors, overcome with fear, could only praise the
God of heaven." Ap. 11 ; 11-13

" In my vision, when he broke the sixth
seal, there was a violent earthquake
and the sun went as black as coarse

64

sackcloth; the moon turned red as blood all over ...." (Ap. 6:12)

" My Voice will be heard and My enemies will tremble and beat their breasts."

" They said to the mountains and the rocks, 'Fall on us and hide us away from the One who sits on the throne and from the anger of the Lamb. (Ap. 6:16)

3. 4. 95

My Heart is your Abode, never forget this! My child, I who am the Supreme High Priest tell you: love My priests and pray for them; now listen and write this: I will instruct your

Excerpts from Notebook 78

3 April 95, continued from NB 77 p.64 . . . My Word Restores...
Need My Holy Spirit As Much As You Need Air

✠ Ask My Holy Spirit to reveal to you the hidden sense of My Parables and My Proverbs and the prophecies of your time

✠ The New Heavens And The New Earth

✠ Allow My Holy Spirit to turn your soul into another Paradise, a New Earth...We (The Holy Trinity) will come into Our Garden and rest among your virtues

✠ The New Heavens? My Holy Spirit will govern you...the Word will be given to you to express thoughts and speech as I would have you think and speak

✠ This earth and heaven will disappear because the radiant glory of My throne will shine in you all

12 April 95, NB p.13 . . . My Purification Will Be Like A Small Judgment

✠ And it will be with righteousness

Message From Jesus For The USA

✠ Where are you who counted the minutes to be with Me?

✠ So many of you read and read My Messages, but without living them...one moment your heart aflame cries out to Me praise and at the next the flame within you dies down

✠ This Inexhaustible Treasure...kept for these Times when Knowledge and Faith would be despised...when people would be preferring their own pleasure to God

✠ I have for the past years, offered you all that Heaven has to offer

✠ So long as you have no love for your Father in Heaven you cannot love your neighbor and you cannot say you are obeying the Commandments

28 April 95, NB p.27 . . . I Am Determined To Assemble All The Peoples Of The Earth And Instruct Them

- ✠ "The Lord is coming from His Holy Dwelling to console His people and consolidate His Church"
- ✠ Today My Eyes are on a man of good omen...it is he who sprouts from the Eastern Bank who will glorify Me
- ✠ To become a healing balm for My House in the West
- ✠ I decided, out of My Love I have for you, to hurry up My Plan
- ✠ To complete their work of destruction...they will have to remove Peter's Chair
- ✠ This hour of great iniquity and great distress has already come upon you

1 May 95, NB p.42 . . . I Was Treated As A Blasphemer

- ✠ They judged Me by human standards as they judge you today
- ✠ On the Judgment Day, all those who...sneered at you will be struck with remorse for having rejected My Inexhaustible Treasure

10 May 95, NB p.51 . . . I Will Hasten The Day Of My Return

- ✠ The three and a half years are already upon you
- ✠ It will appear to you that I have abandoned you all...as though the two Beasts proved the stronger
- ✠ To My Abels I say...I know you by name and you know Me...in Me be rooted

12 May 95, NB p.61 . . . I, Jesus, Will Always Be Your Protection

- ✠ Do not be astonished the way I have spread My Message...every heart conquered while you speak sanctifies you
- ✠ Like a lamp, keep it alight and shining...many will see the <u>Way</u> and will understand that I am their Source of Life...and in this light that I am shedding on them they will learn the only <u>Truth</u> that is:

1

generation so that when they read My
Book* they will understand it;
Altar, allow Me to place on you
My Knowledge, this Inexhaustible Treasure
of My Sacred Heart so that men out of
every people, race, language and nation
may come forward and serve themselves;
and when they do, I will revive them
and brighten their eyes; for My Word
restores; if anyone loves My Word let
him come forth, if anyone loves Me he

* The Holy Bible

2

will keep My Word, and My Father will
love him, and We shall come to him
and make Our home with him; need My
Holy Spirit as much as you need air to
breathe; ask My Holy Spirit who is the
Giver of Life to come to you and do
fresh wonders in your soul .... ask My
Holy Spirit to reveal to you the hidden
sense of My parables and My proverbs
and the prophecies of your time;
a city* cannot be built without

* symbolic word for 'ourself.'

3

foundations *[1] for there would be no set-
tling of My Holy Spirit within it ; come
and learn: the New Heavens and the
New Earth will be when I will set My
Throne in you for I will give water
from the well of Life free to anybody
who is thirsty *[2]; allow My Holy Spirit
then to draw you into My Kingdom and
into Eternal Life ; let evil win no more
power over you to die ; if it was necessary

---

* Meaning, abandonment to God so that God
becomes our foundation. *[2] Ap. 21 : 6

4

I would lay down My life again at
any moment and without hesitation, to
save you; allow My Holy Spirit to cultivate
your soil and make a terrestrial Eden
in you, let My Holy Spirit make a
New Earth to prosper in you your soil
so that your first earth, that was
the devil's property, wears away; then
once again My Glory will shine in you
and all the divine seeds sown in you
by My Holy Spirit will sprout and grow
in My divine Light; allow My

5

Holy Spirit, to come to you as a roaring
fire and purify you by burning all the
dry plants*¹ remaining in you and replace
them with celestial seedlings and delightful
vineyards²*; then from that day onward
I Myself shall be their keeper .... let your
old earth that is nothing else but devastation and ruin now call out to Me and
I shall take pity on your disgrace .... your
few remaining trees now are dry and broken

*¹ dry plants, means : bad habits, sins.
²* These heavenly plants are : virtues.

6

ready for firewood only, so allow My Holy
Spirit to turn your soul into another
Paradise, a New Earth where We* would
make Our Home in you; for see, winter
is past, and the flowers appear on your
soil; see? the vineyard is forming its
first flowers giving out their fragrance;
this *is* Our Paradise, Our Heaven; We
will come into Our Garden to gather
all its fruits; We will come into Our
Garden and rest among your virtues

* *The Most Holy Trinity.*

7

which will be like fountains, wells of living water, lush valleys of all the incense-bearing trees, pastures and vineyards, mountains of myrrh; for humility pleases Us and love delights Us; peace honours Us, and joy enchants Us, why, all the fruits are the virtues that are agreeable in Our Eyes; allow then My Holy Spirit to discipline you and show you that sound teaching is life; make room for My Holy Spirit to take root in the middle of your soul

8

and plant Himself there, there where
a thousand briars and thorns used to
be, My Holy Spirit will be the Tree of Life
in you, and My Kingdom which you will
obtain by My graciousness will lead you
to obtain incorruptibility and the deity to
have eternal life; compare yourself,
Vassula, now, with your old self; see?
see how My Holy Spirit turned your
old earth into a New Earth? and
how only His seeds can yield good fruits
in abundance? and that without His

9

Presence your soul would have remained uncultivated, dry and a land of drought?

What about the New Heavens, Lord?

the New Heavens? they too will be inside you, when My Holy Spirit will govern you in holiness; My Holy Spirit, consort of My Throne will shine in your darkness like a splendid sun in the sky, because the Word will be given to you to express thoughts and speech as I would wish you to think and speak, everything expressed will be in accordance with My

:10

Image and thought; everything you will do
will be to Our likeness because the
Spirit of your Father will be speaking in
you. and your New Universe will march
with My Holy Spirit to conquer the rest
of the stars * for My Glory and those
who had not observed My Law and
were fully drawn away like a passing
shadow into darkness, never knowing
the hope and holiness I was reserving
for your times ; the New Heavens,

* Symbolic for ' people '

11

Altar, will be when My Holy Spirit will be poured out to you all from above, from the highest heaven; yes, I will send My Spirit in you to make a heaven out of your soul, so that in this New Heaven I may be glorified thrice ♡ and as the paths, of those who received My Holy Spirit, will be straightened so will their darkness and gloom too be enlightened and restored into blazing stars illuminating their darkness for ever and ever; soon, this

12

earth and heaven will disappear because
the radiant glory of My Throne will
shine in you all; I, Jesus, tell you:
I, the High Priest, from the highest
heaven call you to come and join Me
by approaching My Throne of Grace;
it is within your reach ♡ come to Me
and you will inherit My Kingdom in
Heaven ♡

♡   IΧΘΥΣ 🐟

13

12. 4. 95

My Lord?

I Am; peace be with you; will you write with Us* today?

Only if You want me Lord.

We want .... if you remain with Us, little one, you will make good progress, so, will you, you who belong to the Most Holy Trinity serve Us? by serving Us you will be obeying Us and glorifying Us;

I will serve You most gladly.

* Jesus is speaking in the Presence of God the Father and the Holy Spirit

14

make Us known the way We have come
to you, then allow Us to sing Our New
Song* through your mouth; those who are
still not contaminated by the powers of
the world will be drawn to Us in Our
Imperishable Light; today We are sending
you like a fiery flame to revive this flick-
ering flame in each heart that is almost
extinct; — Our Presence through this Call
is: forgiveness; Our Presence among you is:
kindness and tenderness, but soon

* The Messages.

15

My Voice will be heard as a clap of thunder among you; — My Voice will be this of justice; I will come to purify the earth; My purification will be like a small judgement and it will be with righteousness;

Message from Jesus to the U.S.A.

say to them this: even though I personally led many safely back to faith through My Call, the earth continues to pine away with rebellion, withering away, because of its drought; if My Eyes, in these

16

days never cease to shed tears of blood it
is because so many of you whose eyes have
seen My Glory, My Mercy and My powerful
intervention in these past years are still
tempted today to look back on what I
vowed to destroy! where are you, you who
counted the minutes to be with Me?
where is your eagerness you once had to
defend My Name and hold it holy? you
who were far away from My Heart
and who came to Me saying: " I am
sickly;" and whom I healed, you have

17

again tuned your ear back to apathy;
in My distress I call, but so many
of you spurn all My warnings!
" deliver My Messages to all the cities so
that they change their lives," I say,
but no sooner do I call than My Voice
is drowned by this yawning darkness that
inhabits My cities .... am I worth <u>so
little</u> in your eyes? I who breathed in
you a living spirit, am I not worth more
for you? so many of you read and
read My Messages but without living them

18

because you read, My children, without understanding*; at one moment your heart aflame
cries out to Me praises and at the next
the flame within you dies down;

— as tenderly as a father who treats
his children I have treated you and have
revealed to your heart this Inexhaustible
Treasure that had been hidden for generations
and was kept for your Times, these Times
when Knowledge and Faith would be

* Many important prophecies in these messages were
accomplished but no one noticed.

19

despised because of the coldness of the world, My Treasure was reserved for the end of times you are now living in, when people would be preferring their own pleasure to God, rendering themselves to every evil than to good; I am pouring out on you My Inexhaustible Treasure from My Sacred Heart like cascades of streams, over mountains and into valleys to make you strong in your love and ready for My Kingdom; I have been like a spring gushing in ravines, running down between the mountains, attracting

20

the thirsty ; I have, for the past years
offered you all that heaven has to offer, so
tell Me, what could I have done more
to save you that I have not done? My
children, I have given you My Law in
the beginning to keep you alive ; My Law
to this day is not kept because you do
not live in the love of God ; so long
as you have no love for your Father in
Heaven you cannot love your neighbour and
you cannot say you are obeying the
Commandments ; so long as what you

21

were taught in the beginning is not alive in you, you are still not rooted in Me; how can you say: " I live in Jesus and in my Father;" have you not heard that on the two greatest Commandments hang the whole Law? I ask you solemnly, " what gain is it for a person to have won the whole world and to have lost the gift of love?" to have lost the gift of love is to have lost the knowledge of God, for if any - one is without love for the Father, he is breaking all the Commandments; I tell

22

you, if your love goes no deeper than what
it is now and does not grow you will never
be able to get into My Kingdom; learn to
glorify the Father and love Him so that
the Father and I make Our home with
you; learn to long and desire the Father
so that your life becomes an unceasing
prayer; if you say you are from God,
then love one another just as much as I
love you so that you live a True Life in
God ♡ have your minds not perceived My
Glory all these years I have been teaching

23

you? I will soon return to you, so do not venture to say: " I have still time to progress;" come now and repent! the fruit of repentance is: Love; so come now and learn to be gracious in your love for your heavenly Father; learn to love not only your neighbour but also those whom you consider as your enemies; if you are merciful to them so will your Father in heaven show you mercy; in My House-hold I have only love;

I have called you by your name to

24

give you Hope; I have opened My Sacred Heart and offered you all My Wealth and Treasures I had hidden over centuries; I have descended from My Throne to be among you with My Heart in My Hand to offer you all this Treasure that is within it; then, when I opened My Mouth and have spoken, you were lost in amazement over My perfect beauty; to stir your love and to rouse you, I breathed on you My delicate fragrance of perfume; in the youth of your conversion you

25

opened your heart freely to Me and asked
Me to conduct you with My Shepherd's
staff, and so I did; of the flock I
pastured very few remained in the fold;
your resistance to wickedness did not
hold; your feet progressively wandered
away from My Heart and you
hastened your steps towards spite and
deceit .... fastidious you have become and
brambles and thorns choked the little
love which was growing and which was
My delight and My honour; how can

26

you say your eyes observe My Commandments
when unsparingly you put your neighbour
to the proof? My Father and I
have journeyed all the way from Heaven
to remind each one of you to open your
hearts to receive Us before My visible
passage on this earth; pray that this
Hour will not find you unaware with
a heart of stone; pray so that this
Hour will not find your spirit void ♡
come to your King with an open
heart and you too will share His

27

Royal Table which is: love;

$$I X \Theta Y \Sigma$$

28. 4. 95

Vassula, let Me sing to you My friend
the canticle I have in My Heart!
write: O My people, My friends, My
kin, your Lord will come and rest
in your heart; you will be renewed
in My Presence for I am determined to
surround you all with songs of deliverance;
I am determined to assemble all the
peoples of the earth and instruct them;

28

My New Song is written so as to honour My
Name ♡ have you not heard
that My intentions are : Salvation
for mankind ? My Plan holds good
for ever and the intentions of My
Heart from age to age;
 listen House of the East! do not
stay deaf to My cries! you waited
for My Sovereignty, beloved House of the
East to descend from the highest
heaven to rescue you and now I tell
you: morning by morning you will grow

29

on your throne, for, see, from your land
will sprout a Shoot of hope, a Shoot of
righteousness and of perfect peace and the
inhabitants of this House will spread peace
everywhere .... daughter of My Eastern House,
declare this with cries of joy, go and proclaim My Words, say,

"the Lord is coming from His
holy dwelling, to console His people
and consolidate His Church;"
today My Eyes are on a man of good
omen and the crown will be given to him;

30

it is he who sprouts from the Eastern
Bank who will glorify Me .... and My
angels will descend with the royal insignia
in their hands and dress him for the throne
as a ruler ♡ ah Vassula! dance and
shout with joy for this day is ever so near
I am already taking action here and now
to bring this day of festival* upon you
so that all the past misfortunes will be
replaced by joy. House of Tradition
have you not heard? have you not
yet understood that from your House

* Jesus means Unity.

31

I will be thrice glorified? have you not
heard that I bestowed heaven's blessings
on your Shoot? just as once you were a
curse among many nations, so I mean
to raise you to become a healing balm
for My House in the West and a blessing
for the nations ♡ House of the East!
a victorious Shoot is sprouting to raise
My House into one; My lips quiver with
emotion and My Heart sings for the
anointed one..... and the abyss roars with
rage at the sound of his footsteps,

32

because My House will be one; the Western House and the Eastern House will live as one because My Name will be their bond, clothing them in perfect peace, integrity and love; My New Name will be the royal insignia between these two Houses ....

this will happen soon and in your time, so do not say, "the Lord takes His time again," I have said to you that I decided, out of My Love I have for you, to hurry up with My Plan; I intend to trample together with

33

My Army, on My Enemy* and on the two Beasts* quicker than foreseen! come and learn: the leaders of destruction are in fact three demon spirits* forming a triangle, taking a corner each, who lead the entire world into their foul world; drunk with the blood of the saints and all those who witness on My Divinity ♡ don't you see? to complete their work of destruction and crown it with success they will have to

* Satan
*² Ap: 13: 1-18 *³ Ap: 16: 13-14

34

remove Peter's Chair and the one who sits on it; their aim is to destroy My Church ....
but, do not be afraid, I had promised that 'the gates of the underworld can never hold out against it'*¹ ♡ yes, this is what is happening now; <u>the leaders of destruction, glittering in their scholarship's degrees, are foul</u> and their stench has covered the entire world now; they are those of whom Scriptures say: they are able to work miracles*², seducing with their

* Mt 16:18   * 2 Th 2:9

35

ability the ten towers of the world and
from them all the nations of the earth;
all are falling under their spell .... once
their army is complete they will raise
their insignia* and together with the three
foul spirits' forces they will come together
to make war against My Perpetual Sacrifice, this is what Scriptures call:
'the war of the Great Day of God
Almighty ...' (Ap. 16: 14)

---

* I also heard at the same time the word
'banner'.

36

in fact this hour of great iniquity and
great distress has already come upon you,
but I will defeat them, for I am the
Lord of lords and the King of kings;
and heaven together with all the saints,
apostles and prophets will celebrate their
downfall; *1 I shall appear on a white
horse, as a warrior of justice *2 and give
judgement for all of My saints, apostles
and prophets, *3 against the dragon *4,

*1 Ap 18: 20
*2 Ap 19: 11
*3 Ap 18: 20   *4 Satan

37

the Beast, the false prophet alias the second Beast and the three foul spirits,*¹ and with My sword I shall strike each one of them*² and the towers they have built will come tumbling down – that is all the followers of the two Beasts under the name of Scholars! like cut thorns they have now penetrated into My Body, but I will extirpate each one of them and burn them in the fire*⁵, and My

---

*¹ Demon spirits. (Ap. 16 : 13) *⁴ Read Ap. 19 : 11-21
*² Ap 19 : 20

38

Breath shall devour the rest of them
like fire .... since nothing can be hidden
from My Eyes, I tell you that over each
nation the Beast and his like have set
a governor, one of their own, who established their authority even over every blade
of grass ;- I am with you to teach you
how to understand; write :
already the second Beast, servant to
the first, shows his immense power by
dragging constantly stars* from the sky

　　* Virtuous souls

39

and dropping them to the earth like figs;
listen and understand: his*[1] power will reach
"right up to the armies of heaven and will
fling armies and stars to the ground,
and trample them underfoot; he will even
challenge the power of that army's Prince;
and will abolish the Perpetual Sacrifice
and overthrow the foundation of His sanctuary";*[2] these are the ones who once were
and are no more; these are the ones

*[1] The power of the beast
*[2] Dn 8: 10-11

40

that ceased to be; the armies of heaven and the stars were once My Own but decided to part from Me and become associates with the beast; "they are all of one mind in putting their strength and their powers at the beast's disposal";* they are selling Me every day and are profaning Me in My Perpetual Sacrifice, in the Blessed Sacrament of My Divine Love; see? see what great disorder is coming? so now

* Ap 17:13

41

let your voice go out through all the
earth and My Message to the ends of
the world; have My Peace to work
with peace; praise Me for giving a new
life to your soul ....

Glory be to God; I thank You, with
all my heart I thank You. I have been
revived and You have given me a heart of
flesh, my flesh has bloomed once more;
By choosing me, You raised me to enjoy
Your favour, allowing me to live in Your
House, all the days of my life.
Blessed be God who allows me to
enjoy every hour His sweetness, His tenderness and His graces. The Word of God
is Life. Teach my tongue to proclaim
Your goodness and praise Your Holy
Name, for ever and ever. Amen.

42

come, I bless you; I will keep nourishing you and I will look after you; ♡

ΙΧΘΥΣ 🐟

1. 5. 95

My Lord: may Your Holy Name be held glorious for ever. My heart flutters with joy at Your Presence and I rejoice in Your favour; and everything You order me to do I try promptly to carry out. In Your Presence I experience the sweetness of Your Heart, and Your teachings which are: Life, Joy, Peace, Love and Sanctity. They are a Song for our soul, revealing the hidden mysteries of Your Kingdom.

But when I sing Your Love Song with all my heart and voice and bless Your Name thrice holy, they come crashing upon me calling me 'a wrong-doer;

43

they sit on a judicial bench with a
scepter of falsehood, always trying
to invent new accusations; when will
they renounce their fault?

lean on Me, I am with you; let not
those things worry your heart; I am in
charge of My Church, so never feel discouraged; Vassula My flower, remember:
there was no one to instruct you but Myself; I came to teach you and through
you others; I am your Teacher and I
love you; learn from Sweetness itself
learn, My pupil, without self-interest and

44

pass on without reserve; look, My child, I am known not to stand in awe of human greatness; if these became judges and omit to observe holy things holily will be adjudged themselves as unholy; have you forgotten that I was treated as a blasphemer and I was condemned for this reason? so why are you surprised to be judged as someone who uses per-verted and abusive language? they judged Me by human standards as they judge you today; My child, fear not, lo tedhal!

45

on the Day of Judgement they will come
trembling in front of My Throne to the
reckoning of their sins unless they repent
before their day ; their ruthless Judgement
on you will be ruthless as well on
them ; their accusations will accuse them ;
I tell you, Vassula, one day, in My
courts and on the Judgement Day, all
those who accused you and sneered at you
will be struck with remorse for having
rejected My Inexhaustible Treasure from
which their spirit could have acquired

46

Wisdom and won My friendship, this
friendship that would have led them into
the beauty of My Sovereignty and Splendour
and the intimacy of their God; your
accusers will look at you and say, as Scriptures say: " this is the one we used to laugh
at once, a butt for our sarcasm, fools
that we were! her life we regarded as
madness .... " and you, My child, will face
every one of those who have oppressed you,
and they will realize how bitter they
made My Cup .... remain with Me in My

47

agony, I need your friendship; pray and say to Me these words:

" my Lord,

may the words of my mouth find favour and consolation for Your

Sacred Heart;

Redeemer of the world,
why do they weave plans against You

over and over again?

Consoler of Your kin,
why do they keep loading You

48

with sorrow and grief?

Friend of mankind,
why do Your Own deny your
wounded Heart
and plant banners of trouble in sin
all through their life?

the heavens openly declare Your Glory
and Your Voice is heard to the
ends of the world calling out:

" return to Me and I will give you

49

a new life for your soul;"

but scorn is what You receive
my Redeemer;
and ah, so many jeer at Your Call,
my Consoler!

Friend of mankind, Perfect Beauty,
Light Thrice Holy,
Your Love is betrayed again,
denied and tested;
Your enemies multiply and their
violence increases;

50

Sacrificial Lamb,

accused by Your accusers,

attacked constantly by Your attackers,

when will You appear on Your horse

as: Warrior for Justice?"

My Own, never leave My Heart, My enemies persecute you but in reality are persecuting Me;* My angel, My child, the Father is sending you to travel for Us and testify, this is why My label is on you;

* Allusion to: Acts 9: 4-5

51

take courage, I am beside you; call Me when you are weary and I will lift you; fill My assemblies and do not be afraid; I am the One who will intervene in times of tyranny practised on you, so be patient;

ΑΡΩ

10. 5. 95

My God, my Lord, make every tongue on earth talk about 'peace', 'reconciliation', 'love,' 'faith' and 'unity'; Send Your Holy Spirit in time, show everyone that You are our Help and Consolation, come and revive what little is left otherwise how would the dead hear about Your marvels in the dark? How would they see Your righteousness if

52

their spirit still lies in the Land of oblivion?
        Your love for me has been so
great, Your mercy fathomless, and
without any merit You have offered
me Wisdom, a priceless gift.... and
You gave me speech to declare Your
Love; *

daughter, open your heart to Me
and tell Me everything....

My soul is troubled....

I am listening....

My opponents are more opponent than ever....
        A brutal clan is at my heels.

listen and understand: I have allotted

* I was not going to the point.

53

you a prophet's seat, so for the rest of
your life you will prophesy and will be
associated with My Works but also with everything they* had to endure; – do not
stand there as if you were suddenly widowed....
find your relief in My Love for I am
with you; have My Peace .... will you
write?

If You want me to, Lord.
I want .... listen and write;
Vassula, I think you have now noticed
how Satan's fortifications are growing
* The prophets

54

stronger, this is why I decided to hasten My Day; let mankind know:

<u>I will hasten the Day of My Return</u>;

I once said to you, not long ago, to hurry up with My Work because you were at the dawn of the great events; then later on I came again to you to tell you that you are facing the great tribulations to come; but now I am telling you: offer Me incense and pray every day so that I may grant you the grace of relief; My daughter,

55

grief is coming, grief is well on its way into My sanctuary; this darkness of iniquity I foretold you; the three and a half years are already upon you; this hour has already been upon you since the beginning of this spring season; your generation has entered the beginning of sorrows and trials, these terrible times of iniquity; the times of abomination and desolation; the hour of shadows and of the Beast; the times thrice cursed by Satan; the hour where he swore to harass My

56

saints and My angels*¹; the times are here when the evil one will send one of his own to change My Law and seasons; it will appear to you then that Sovereignty and Splendour is not around you any more, it will appear to My saints as though My Court is not there to open the books*²; it will seem to you as though I have abandoned you all; it will appear to you all as though the two Beasts proved the stronger but this will only be for a short time

*¹ messengers   *² Justice from God

57

until My Return; I shall come like a thief .... I shall suddenly come upon you to break the sceptre of falsehood, and the earth will tremble; with just one of My glances I will make the rebellion of every nation quake and I will dissolve, this rebellion that brought this Apostasy down on you like a plague, in My Flames; I will dislodge the apostates and the thrones of those who changed seasons, My Tradition, and who passed their life contradicting

58

and opposing My Abels *¹ and the one *² who
shepherds them; I will stride the earth and
will not leave one stone unturned, for I
have sworn to devour with My Flames all
that does not come from Me and that
defiled My Image; — for years now I
have been sending you new apostles to be
among you to remind you of My Law and
to listen to My warnings *³ they
have been prophesying since many years

*¹ The loyal priests
*² John Paul Ⅱ   *³ Jesus sighed.

59

now, but so very few listened .... I have
sent them to remind you to apply My Law
and practise kindness and compassion towards
each other; I have sent them to be My
Echo, reminding you, generation, to repay
evil with love and to love one another,
but to this day your hearts are closed and
harder than ever .... you do not apply My
Law nor to My requests; your hearts

continue to plan evil against one
another and are adamant rather than
listen to My Calls that I had made known

60

by My Spirit through My new apostles of
your days .... since you have, generation,
done all these things that I abhor and
you have not practised love and peace, but
rebellion instead, you will receive according
to your measure .... what you have har-
vested you shall now reap ....

Is there no word of hope for the faithful,
the Abels as You call them, my Lord?

to My Abels I say: I will make My Justice
known ♡ do not be afraid; I know you
by name and you know Me; always be

61

wanting peace with all people ; make sure
that no one disobeys his leader so that no
root of rebellion begins in him; continue in
My grace and do not harden your hearts ;
I am your Hope and in Me be rooted ;
I will look after you while iniquity is
rising at its peak; I love you all, eternally; be one in My Name ♡ IXΘΥΣ ⳿⳽⳽⟿

12. 5. 95

Scriptures say : " if a property has no fence,
it will be plundered." * Lord, let Your
arms be my fence, protect me, I who am
Your property. Do not allow the Plunderer
to step inside Your property and make a
devastation out of it, otherwise I will

* Si. 36: 25

62

end up in flames!

I, Jesus, will always be your protection*,
do not lose the Peace I have given you ....
your food is to do My Will; by grace I
have lifted you to be My bearer; and by
grace you will complete your work with Me;
do not be astonished the way I have
spread My Message; open your ear, daughter,
and hear the 'sound' of My Footsteps, I
am not far from you*²; work for My Church,
I, Jesus Christ, prepared for you water to

* Jesus used the word 'protection' instead of 'protector'
*² Jesus means: His Return.

63

drink and relieve you; I know that it is hard, My beloved, to be crossing this ruthless desert, but I am with you ....

(The Eternal Father speaks now)

I, your Heavenly Father bless you; every word you utter about Me, glorifies Me; every heart conquered while you speak sanctifies you .... every blame thrust on you unjustly purifies your soul drawing it closer to Me; should every one, even your dearest friends, abandon you, I will never abandon you; you are My

64

delight; to lead you is also a delight
for Me; — I have entrusted you with My
work, so like a lamp, keep it alight
and shining; your era is obscure, My
child, but by using what I have
preached to you and taught you,
many will see the Way and will understand that I am their Source of Life;
many will be attracted and will enjoy
the light I am giving them, and in
this light I am shedding on them they
will learn the only Truth, that is:

Excerpts from Notebook 79

Message of 12 May 95, continued from NB 78 p.78 . . . That I Am The Only True God, And Jesus Christ, My Only Son

✠ Although you will continue to be a sign of contradiction, you will accomplish your mission with Me

✠ (Blessed Mother), NB p.2

✠ The Almighty's designs are so profound in His Messages (that) many will be healed

✠ Continue to draw every soul into the intimacy of God; attract My children into the Divine Love Of God

✠ (St. Michael), NB p.4

✠ Every time a soul awakens and finds God, all Heaven rejoices and celebrates

✠ Many times you have made Our joy in heaven increase when in your nothingness you glorify the Almighty by bringing souls to love God

✠ You will learn to bear your trials with astounding joy

29 May 95, NB p.9 (Galilee) . . . My Eyes Never Stopped Following You From The Moment You Were Born

30 May 95, NB p.14 (Bethlehem) . . . Love Is The Way To Heaven

✠ Ask for the gift of love and I will give it to you

✠ My Love Theme is given to all nations

✠ Open your hearts and I will heal them

✠ What I see in this generation...wickedness that surpassed the wickedness of the demons

✠ When the sinner renounces sin to become law-abiding and honest, he deserves to live...he shall not die

✠ My Eyes shed tears of Blood and My Eyelids run with weeping...so very few repent

✠ The slightest sign of regret for your sins, and I will forgive and forget

15 June 95, NB p.19 . . . Enter Into The Mystery Of My Heart And Receive My Peace

✠ Evangelize with love for Love

✠ Resent, My child, all that leads to evil

✠ I burn with a desire...to see My Church united and one

✠ Humility and love are the keys to unity

✠ Bow down that you may see My Will; lower your voice so that you hear Salvation speaking to you from the heights of glory

✠ It is in the splendor of the Truth that you will...make everyone recognize themselves as part of one body

✠ I in My turn will multiply your remedies and cure you completely...I will bring your heart in a revolution of love such as your era has never seen

✠ Pray for the...East and the West to join together...a pair of hands...belonging to the same body...when will those Hands of My Body lift Me over the Altar...together?

✠ Dedicate My treasure of My Sacred Heart to the whole earth

✠ I will cure many more through these messages

I, Jesus, Love You, Have My Blessings

that I am the only true God, and
Jesus Christ, My only Son, Lord of
Lords, the Messiah; My teachings will
give them a better knowledge of My Word;
I have told you all this so that you
may find peace in Me and consolation;
remember too, My daughter, that in times
of danger I will lift you; I guarantee
to you that you will reach the end of
the road I have laid out for you;
although you will continue to be a sign
of contradiction, you will accomplish your

2

mission with Me, and you will glorify Me.....

(Our Lady speaks)

'pethi mou',* ' the Almighty's designs are so profound in His Message that many will be healed. My Son is with you; I am also with you; I have come to reassure you of My assistance; .... add a smiling face to all your gifts *² .... continue to

* ' In Greek: 'My child.'

*² Our Lady in saying these words to me was smiling and had a slight tone of teasing because of my so downcast face! — Immediately while saying this to me, not only did my face brighten up, but I found myself laughing with delight.

3

please God by prophesying and showing to every nation what He has truly revealed to you so that all those who listen to you may acknowledge Him as Saviour and as Love .... continue to draw every soul into the intimacy of God; attract My children into the Divine Love of God; and you, My daughter, grow in His Spirit and never feel downcast; expand His Message as you do now and remain reassured; God-is-with-you .....

(St Michael the Archangel speaks now)

4

Vassula, have you not read : " like a young man marrying a virgin, so will the One who formed you wed you.... and as the bride-groom rejoices in his bride so does your God rejoices in you "; know this, Vassula, every time a soul awakens and finds God, all heaven rejoices and celebrates as men are happy and celebrate when they are invited at a wedding, so it is when heaven celebrates .... I wish to tell you that many times you have made Our joy in heaven increase when in your nothingness you glorify the Almighty by bringing souls

5

to love God .... so do not fear; and now write again what had been inscribed on a tablet and in a book long ago but remained to be a witness forever so that it may serve in the time to come:

" this is a rebellious people, they are lying sons, sons who will not listen to Yahweh's orders; to the seers they say, 'see no visions'; to the prophets, 'do not prophesy the truth to us; tell us flattering things; have illusory visions; turn aside from the way, leave the path, take

6

the Holy One out of our sight;"* in a
short time in a very short time the
Holy One will come as a flame of devouring
fire and surprise the haughty but the lowly
will rejoice for having put their hope in
Him; Salvation comes from above, Sovereignty leans down from heaven to be gracious
to you; therefore, anyone who listen to His
Calls and prepares himself by repenting will
be like the sensible man who built his
house on rock; the Lord is your Rock ♡

* Is 30 : 9 - 11

7

I am the guardian of your house * and the Lord the foundation of your house .... and now, daughter of the Most High, one advice: remain rooted in God, in His Love and no attack will be able to shake you; remain united in the Most Holy Trinity and you will shake your accusers by your firm resistance to temptations; remain in the Most Holy Trinity and you will have in you the strength for this battle to

---

* The word "house" can be understood as 'soul'. (Dn 12 : 1) "At that time Michael will stand up, the great prince who mounts guard over your people ...."

8

hold on till the end, never giving in;
you will obtain enough grace from God's
own glorious power so that you accomplish your mission; everything will be done
in perfect harmony and you will learn to
bear your trials with astounding joy;
glory to Him who is pouring on you His
Graces to maintain you in His Light,
His Mercy to sustain His Justice, His
Strength to make you live according to
His Commandments! Yahweh is
just and good, full of pity for his

9

children, faithful and true for all times,
unsparingly He offers His gifts and shares
His Treasures drawing each soul into His
Heart; have no fear; Yahweh-is-with-
you ♡   Saint Michael the Archangel

                          of God, Yahweh;

                Holy - Land - Galilee   29. 5. 95
(Late at night in Galilee.)
I said: "I will go to my Lord's territory
and seek His Face." My heart has
said of You: " Seek His Face and enjoy
the sweetness of His smile, answer His
Call, answer His Call to His Land."
      My Lord, King! Joy of my heart; Spring
of my soul, my heart exults in Your
Presence and my soul rejoices in Your

10

abundant Love! My only Love come and
display Your marvellous kindness in this
tormented nation; Your Presence will bring
them Hope; Your Eyes are known to be
fixed on what is right, and Your judgement is true. Joy of my heart, are
You around or are You hiding from me?
are You listening at this ever so faint
appeal?

My Vassula, do you know that My
Eyes never stopped following you from
the moment you were born? I Am
all (yes*¹!) the time with you and (*¹yes!)
present!.....*²come, just a small

* He asked me to underline the word three times
just so as to emphasize it. Jesus was
really stressing His words. *² A short silence.

11

prayer*; say:

blessed be Your Name,

O You who hear my prayer!

blessed are You my Lord

who removed my soul from the pit,

You have looked upon me from

the heights and humbled my soul

(from my mother's womb with fasting;) (this
sentence is for me only)

* The way Jesus said ' come, just a small
prayer' was one of His typical ways of expression, after a short silence to change tone and
attitude saying what followed with a rush as
though we had to hurry and get going, and at
the same time treating me as a weak child and He,
taking a paternal attitude.

12

Blessed be Your Graciousness
who drew me in Your Heart
to save me and set me free;
God, You are my salvation,
my riches, my sight and my life,
You who daily enchant my soul
and rejoice my heart with Your
Presence,
allow Me to profit from Your Presence:
peace, integrity, love and a
spirit of forgiveness,
let every fibre of my heart

13

proclaim with love Your Glory;

hear my prayer now that I am

Your passing guest in Your country

and answer me;   amen

.... this is all;   let My other guests*

too, whom I bless, read this prayer;

all I ask is: love - love - love!

Jesus is My Name ic ♡

                                    and Jifna!
(— I was called to witness in Ramallah, Bir Zeit, Bethlehem
* I was accompanied by 20 pilgrims, most of
   them Greek orthodox who came from the island
of Rhodos, and some from Athens. Some came from
France, Switzerland, Holland and Puerto Rico.
   The others apart from fr. O Carroll were from
Bethlehem, R. Catholics. (This message was read out
in the boat on the Sea of Galilee.)

14

Back to Bethlehem 30.5.95

Vassula, I am with you and all I ask is love; tell them and let them all understand that love is the way to heaven love conquers hearts and enlarges My Kingdom; love is the key to end up this Apostasy; love is given to you freely, ask for the gift of love and I will give it to you; My Love Theme* is given to all nations and those who want to hear it will hear it; ♡ pray, pray, pray but do it with

* This message

15

love; open your hearts and I will heal
them; repay evil with love, seek good
and Goodness from above will answer you
and turn you into Our likeness. I
know all things and I observe all things
and what I see in this generation is
not according to Our likeness; insolence,
violence, greed, vainglory, wickedness that
surpassed the wickedness of the demons,
rebellion against Me and all that is holy,
and all the vices that can bring your
soul to ruin are what most of this

16

generation practises; every kind of wrong -
doing is sin .... lift your eyes and
be eager to find Me and do not fall
victims to worldly beauty, for the worship
of that sort of beauty is the cause of
so much evil, to crown now your wickedness you embroidered your plan to the
likeness of the beast and together*, generation, you will commit your crime :

to abolish My Perpetual Sacrifice
and erect in its place the disastrous
abomination.

* With the beast

17

have you not heard : " when the upright man renounces his integrity to commit sin and dies because of this ! he dies because of the evil that he himself has committed, but when the sinner renounces sin to become law- abiding and honest, he deserves to live; he has chosen to renounce all his previous sins; he shall certainly live, he shall not die; " * My Eyes shed tears of Blood and My Eyelids run with weeping, O what sorrow you cause Me, generation!

* Ez : 18 : 26-28

18

because Death has climbed into your house
and you do not realize it! so very few
repent .... but most of you, generation, are
not saying what you ought to : you do
not repent of your wickedness saying :
'what have I done with my life, my soul
and my heart?' the slightest sign of regret for your sins, and I will forgive
and forget; happy the ones who meditate
on My words and My appeal and reason
with good sense, they shall be saved;
I bless you with all My Heart I bless

19

you ♡ ic

15. 6. 95

Your Word, my King, is a healing balm,
  when my life was more ignoble than clay,
Your Word was uttered in my ear and
  the invisible swiftly became visible and
like a world unknown to me, like a light
unknown to the blind, everything suddenly
was shining with brilliant light. Like brightly
blazing stars that illuminate the heavens by
night, Your Word gave me sight to enter
  into Your Mystery. I bless You, my Lord,
for Your Love now is visible before my eyes
  bringing my soul to live in loyalty to You
for ever and ever.

yes! enter into the mystery of My Heart
and receive My Peace ;   flower, never
substitute your time of writing with other

20

things; you have <u>all</u> day and I will be pleased if you come to Me in meditation; remember: love is always patient, so be patient too; do not run ahead of Me as you have done in these past days.... love, true love, will endure trials, set-backs and the lot; have Me as first and above all; evangelize with love for love and glorify Me; resent, My child, all that leads to evil and immerse yourself into all that is good and holy and which will lead you into eternal

21

life; I am Holy and Good...* — I burn with a desire....

Which desire, my Lord?

to see My Church united and one..... pray for unity and do not listen to those who do not want unity; the Divider keeps them separated and agressive in their spirit; — anyone who does not work sincerely and with all his heart for unity is seriously grieving My Holy Spirit;

* Suddenly our Lord stopped, and with another tone of voice, like someone who wants to confide his secret said what followed.

22

I implore those who assemble to lead My
Church into one to impress on their minds
those words :

— <u>humility and love</u> —

humility and love are the keys to unity;
it is not the eloquence of speech nor
the lengthy discourse that will lead them
to unity; it is not their exchange of
praise on one another that will lead My
Church into one; all these things weary
Me .... devastation and ruin have penetrated
into My Sanctuary, so what praise can

23

they exchange on one another? where is their honour? <u>bow down</u> that you may see My Will; <u>lower your voice</u> so that you hear Salvation speaking to you from the heights of glory; it is <u>in</u> your conversion that your heart will hear Me and lead My Church into one, unifying My Body; it is <u>in</u> the splendour of the Truth that you will fragrance again and will make everyone recognize themself as part of one body; it is in the sharing that you will

24

lead everyone close to one another; for
this you need to change in your heart
and flower with conversion; if you do these
things and wash your heart clean of your
sin, I in My turn will multiply My
remedies and will cure you entirely; I
will bring upon you a spiritual growth
which will bring the remnant of My creation
to abide under your roof; if you,
you who ceased to be, allow My
Holy Spirit, the Giver of Life, to entice
you, I will bring your heart in a

25

spiritual revolution of love such as your era has never seen .... ah .... daughter, pray for the house of the East and the West to join together, like two hands when joined in prayer, a pair of hands, similar, and in beauty when joined together pointing towards heaven when in prayer; let those two Hands, belonging to the same body work together and share their capacity and resources with each other .... let those two Hands lift Me together, ah .... when will those

26

Hands of My Body lift Me over the Altar, holding Me together? * O come! I do not want lengthy discourses, anyone who wants to be first and best among you must be slave to all; I am here! look to yourself! and there are endless treasures in My Heart; so do not say: "where, where can I find my answers?" equip yourself with this treasure of My Heart and you will bring together

---

* Christ means over Mass, during the Consecration of His Body.

27

those that have been led astray and I
will reign over them all and you will
dedicate My treasure of My Sacred Heart
to the whole earth;   –   and
you, daughter: by giving Me your time
you please Me and it honours Me;
loving Me rejoices Me and glorifies Me;
desiring Me infatuates Me; the amount
given to Me from your heart is the
amount you will be given back from
My Throne; My grace is upon you and
My Hand on yours .... rest in Me; I

28

love you and the Father loves you for loving Me;

                    I love You Love ....

I will cure many more through these messages; do your part, My Vassula, and I will complete your work in My Divinity; come, I will be with you while you do your other small duties *; I, Jesus, love you, have My blessings

A ☧ Ω

---

* Housework of course ....